Walking A Mile In Someone Else's Shoes: Vocational Grieving, Transition and Recovery

By Rebekah J. Colson

Copyright © 2018 Rebekah J. Colson
All rights reserved.
ISBN: 9781720037873

Dedication

To my amazing husband Brad, who encouraged me in this endeavor, made space for me to be absent while I traveled for interviews, and cheered me on when I had writer's block. To our four children, who are our legacy and our deepest pride. And to the 50 people who patiently endured my probing questions and made themselves vulnerable through their career transition stories: My heartfelt thanks and gratitude for helping to make my lifelong dream a reality!

CONTENTS

	Acknowledgements	i
1	An Introduction to Vocational Grieving	1
2	An Examination of Greif and Transition	5
3	First Careers: Finding Your Path	12
4	Second Careers: Unique Challenges	42
5	What Are Your Coping Skills?	70
6	Traumas That Create Crossroads	74
7	Fresh Starts: How to Think Outside of the Box	116
8	Retirement Stories and Twilight Adventures	140
9	"And In Conclusion..."	165
	Bibliography	170

Acknowledgements

To John Fisher of C2D Limited who provided the Transition Curve model used throughout this book: thank you for helping me to colorfully illustrate the struggle to adjust over the lifetime of a career! To Lisa Toboz, talented photographer and friend of 25 years: heartfelt appreciation for entrusting your art to the pages of this book and for your writing advice! And to Jeff Schreckengost for designing the cover, you are an artist extraordinaire, I am grateful to benefit.
To Brad Colson, my dear husband, book designer, and patient friend, I couldn't have done this without your artful expertise.
To the authors of "Psychology Applied to Modern Life: Adjustment in the 21st Century" (Weiten, Lloyd, Dunn & Hammer): Chapter Five is in homage to your brilliance!

Chapter 1:
An Introduction to Vocational Grieving

There are many things grieved over a lifetime: lost loves, opportunities, relatives, or friendships that naturally pass from present into past as we graduate university, get married, or start families. There are other things - silently grieved - that can sit in our chest like a small heavy stone. One instance of such grief is the life or the identity that we leave behind as we make vocational transitions. From university to career path, from career path to stay-at-home status, from home to part-time job, from military to civilian life, or from career to retirement: these 'small deaths' are often treated as natural transitions, and are typically not acknowledged nor honored. And the losses can be countless: work friends, a sense of purpose, vocational identity, intellectual discourse or stimulation, money, dating opportunities, validation from peers, opportunities for career advancement, and work team victories. In American society, we are trained to believe that when we make these vocational shifts, we can shed the old skin of a life as casually as a woman slips out of her high heels when she arrives home after a long day of work.

In reality, work transitions (especially abrupt or traumatic ones) are more like a journey. As a person adjusts to a new position, company, or career, the shoes that felt tight, awkward or "wrong" at first should start to soften and feel more comfortable. If they don't, a worker will often either leave and try a new start somewhere else, or stay and suffer in silence.

Women often experience many personal and career interruptions if they marry, or have children, and raise their children; and they transition frequently between university, first jobs, family, and career. Men are more consumed by (career) growth and identity than they are by family life, and so experience less frequent interruptions and consequently, less 'small deaths' (Evers & Sieverding, 2013).

I was compelled to write this book when I realized that men and women, particularly in American society, are not taught how to grieve vocational loss, nor how to handle vocational transitions. Personal and professional development can only progress when we have reached acceptance of the vocational change, also known as the death of the old dream. John M. Fisher, a British psychologist and vocational skills trainer, explores these themes in his theoretical Process, The Personal Transition Curve. The Personal Transition Curve is a Process of vocational adjustment and change that is used by companies and organizations worldwide:

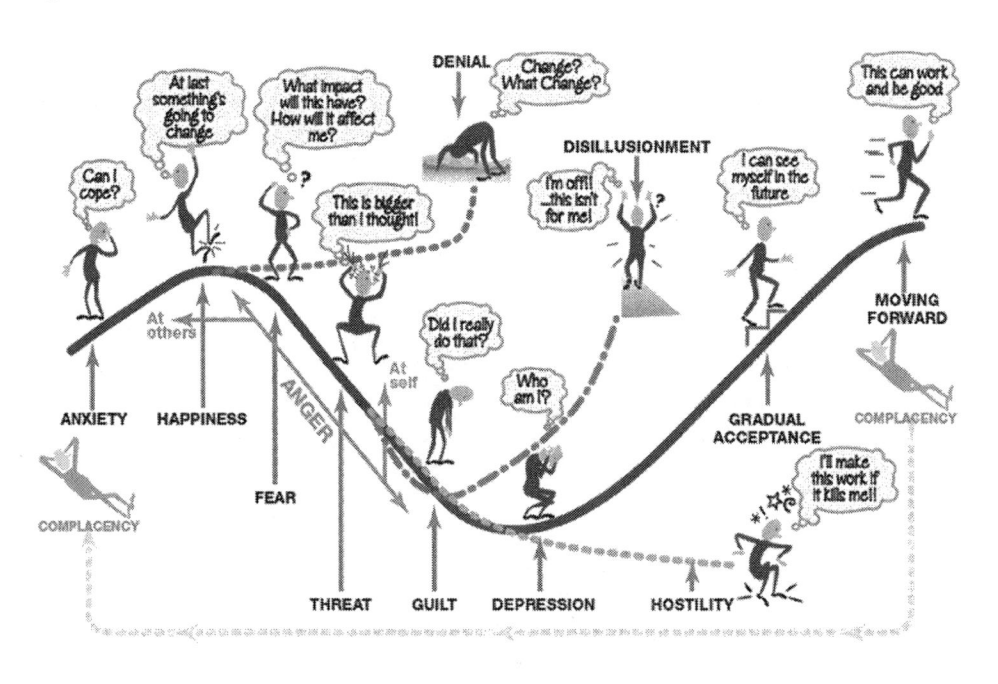

Personal Transition Curve Model courtesy of John M. Fisher, at www.c2d.co.uk; C2D is the company of John Fisher, an experienced Management Development and Soft Skills trainer, coach, facilitator and counsellor who is a Chartered Psychologist working within businesses.

It seems that there is something inherently dishonorable in not naming vocational grief; something inhumane in pretending that the grief does not exist, that slipping into the next set of clothes doesn't feel awkward at first. It is a process of loss, recovery and acceptance, not just one moment in time. There are costs to our emotional, psychological and vocational wellbeing if we ignore the impact of these losses.

What's The Impact of Vocational Transitions?

Many adults experience more than one significant vocational transition in a lifetime. Consequently, marking each transition and being 'in the moment' is important for many reasons, not the least of which is health. Psychological, emotional, physical and spiritual health can all be negatively affected by work transition stress (grief) that is ignored, even when the change is voluntary, expected or a positive decision (Moyle & Parkes, 1999).

In this book, we will examine what vocational grief **is,** and what it looks like. We will illustrate visual examples of the process of vocational transitions, and what is involved in various stages of transitions. We will explore the different types of coping skills, and what their foci are. We will identify the stages of transition, and the types of coping.

We will also see what vocational grieving **could** look like when explored in a more honorable way, and in an "awake" state; instead of sleepwalking our way through these 'small deaths.' We will observe the healthy ways that some individuals used their natural (and professional) support systems to adjust more completely, and the gratitude with which they regard these support systems.

Why would I use the concept of grief as the structure around which to discuss vocational transitions? My curiosity about the topic grew from my observations of those around me, when talking to loved ones and co-workers and neighbors regarding vocational changes and transitions, and their personal experiences. Some of these had gone well, some of these were a more neutral experience, and some transitions were almost exclusively negative ("soul-crushing" was how it was described by a family friend).

Vocational grieving can be confusing, overwhelming, and a private process - which makes it a lonely experience overall. And, especially in the case of most of my male subjects (except for their spouses or partners), it was rare for anyone to check in with them when they experienced job transitions, to make sure that they were adjusting well and processing everything healthfully. Conversations around transition difficulty don't come naturally to men, whereas women tend to verbally process difficulties even if they are introverted ("Stress and Gender Study", 2011). Men are less likely to seek help when their health is affected by work stress, less likely to link poor health to increases in stress, and more likely than women to be diagnosed with high blood pressure, Type 2 diabetes, and heart disease or heart attack ("Stress and Gender Study").

Additional note Any time a * is present next to a person's name, that indicates they have chosen to use a pseudonym for their story. Some interview subjects are still in their jobs as described in their story, or they wanted to be completely honest and preserve their anonymity.

Chapter 2:
An Examination of Grief and Transition

What *is* grief? The etymology of the word grief is Old French, from *grever,* meaning *to afflict, burden, or oppress.* If our grief is held onto too long, is embraced as an extended stage of life, it can burden us psychologically or physically (Romm, 2014). Picture a cardboard boat being gripped tightly by a child sitting at the edge of a pond. He knows that if he holds on to the boat instead of releasing it, that it isn't fulfilling its function. Nevertheless, he continues to grip it and to ponder what he should gain by releasing it, and what he would gain by keeping it.

Grief happens whether we give it permission to exist. When a person takes off the psychological "suit of clothes" that comprises a work identity, the impression of that tie, that belt, those heels last for a little while longer. Whether you immediately put on a new identity, if the transition moment isn't marked and remarked upon, grief can set in.

It can feel like a restlessness; discontent; a lump in the throat; sleeplessness; something lost. It can leave you patting the pockets of your suit coat, wondering what it is that you are forgetting when you leave the house. It can leave you scratching your head, absent minded.

Transition is a change from one state or condition to another, or to **make a change** from one state, place or condition to another. *Transition* can be used as a noun, a verb, or adjective (a transition, to transition, transitional). It implies a fluidity of motion, but in our psychological experiences, transition can be a series of stops, starts, and steps (either forward or backward). Unresolved grief can create hiccups in our transitions, both in work and in our personal lives.

The other mitigating factor in whether a vocational transition goes smoothly is if a concurrent life transition interferes, such as the death of a spouse, divorce, a serious illness or injury. When stressors pile upon each other, the resulting instability or chaos can delay or even retard healthy transition into a new work role.

There are many instances in which a person is grieving a marriage while at the same time adjusting to a new role as primary provider for their children:

Su Logan: Shoulders Back, Chin Up

Su Logan is in her early 50's, a tall, attractive, strong woman who meets with me in my home and takes some time to consider each interview question. Su starts out guarded and then warms up to the subject of transitions, both in work and in her personal life. She doesn't hesitate to tweak and correct any information reflected to her, as she is very interested in her story being told in an authentic and honest way.

Su Logan's youngest son was in kindergarten when their family life came to a screeching halt: her marriage fell apart and her husband moved out. "I spent the next six months in a sort of daze, and then decided to attain some personal focus by going to work part-time at a local bank." The position allowed her to be at home when her two sons were home from school. When her older son was 13, she started working full-time for the bank, knowing that she was working just down the street and able to come home if an emergency arose. Her mom and dad lived on the same block too, so anytime her older son needed non-emergency assistance or just wanted to hang out somewhere else, the two boys walked to their grandparents' house. "I also have many friends in the neighborhood who belong to my Christian group, whom I trusted to keep an eye out for the boys."

Around the same time, Su became financially disentangled from her husband, and she independently paid the bills, while he continued to pay the mortgage on the house. It took her a bit of time to get used to taking over the responsibility of all the bills, and in the emotional turmoil of the unraveling of the marriage, that wasn't always easy. "I also figured that I would have to find a more lucrative full-time job, so that if my husband was ever in financial trouble, I could still provide for the boys."

To that end, Su sought out a position in the mortgage closing industry, but after two years and three different mortgage companies (because of increases in interest rates, etc., mass layoffs at closing companies were common), she knew she needed a better long-term plan. She had reached the Disillusionment stage of Fisher's Process, in which a person assesses their current vocation and decides whether to stay and be miserable, or go and find something more suitable:

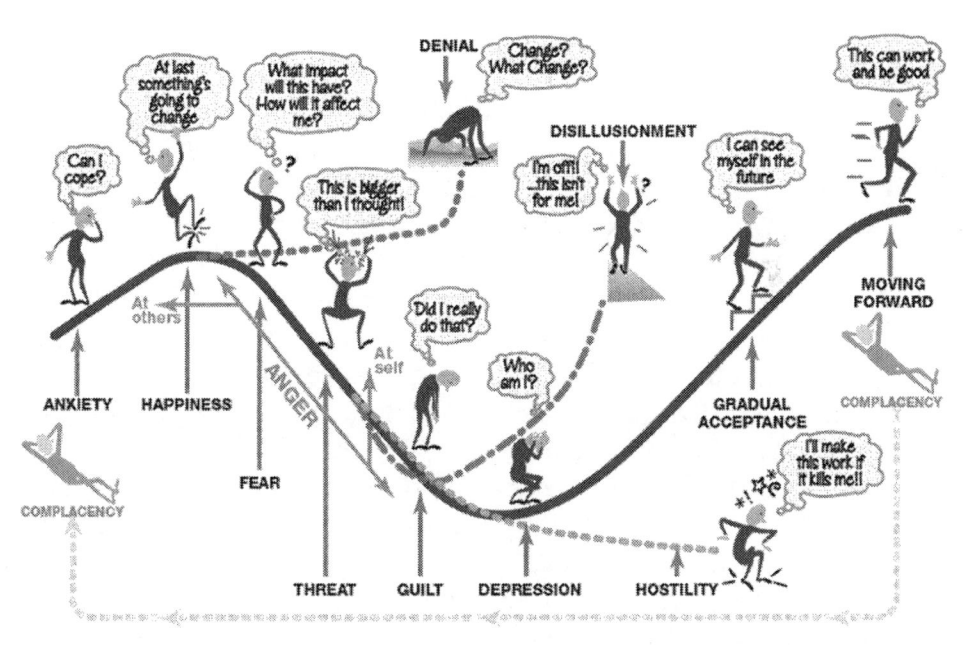

"Because I had a Bachelor's Degree in Business Administration, I decided to go back to working for the state's Department of Human Services, where I worked before my boys were born." She interviewed for a caseworker position in March of 2001, and that year her husband moved to Kentucky. In the middle of all the career decisions, there was still the looming question of when their separation would become a divorce, as Su had taken a markedly responsive (even passive) approach to his lead in the dissolution of their marriage. "I now wish that someone would have come alongside me to mentor me through the divorce process, and looking back, would have had the legalities of child support and divorce formalized in the courts." Her divorce became final two years after she started working full time for the state, which was six or seven years after her husband had moved out.

However, Su did have the foresight to understand that her husband's occasional unemployment or changes in job status would cause fluctuation in financial support of the children, and was proactive in steering her own career path so that her children would always have their needs met. She was in the Gradual Acceptance step of Fisher's Process. Su has now been back at her state job for almost 14 years, and has been promoted to Income Maintenance Casework Supervisor.

"Although my job is tough, and employment politics a constant source of stress, it has provided well for me and my children." Su, age 52, does have some regrets; she feels that she should have gone to nursing school after the separation, that it would have fit her personality and interests better, and would have been a more enjoyable job overall.

Su also feels that she became a single mother at a time when that status was an unusual situation, at least in her demographic (white, suburban, over 40), and she felt like an unanchored ship at times. Her parents and her younger brother were most supportive and understanding; after that, her other two brothers who didn't live as close, and her Christian prayer group's small group members. "I remember feeling like my marital status was so unsure and unusual, that it was almost like people didn't know what to "do" with me."

Su just tried to hunker down and make her sons' lives as normal and stable as possible, and continued with their family plans and traditions like they did before her husband left. They had holidays as planned, went on vacations, and visited with relatives, including her ex's parents. Su accepted her "fate" as a single mother early on, and although she had no mentors to guide her through the social and other types of awkwardness associated with this role, she embraced her new calling in a serious and realistic way. She had transitioned to the Moving Forward stage of Fisher's Process, in both her familial and vocational roles.

What does she miss about being a stay at home mom? "I miss some things, like being able to come alongside the boys for after school activities, giving them a more normative childhood with both parents present in the home, and having a well-rounded family experience." However, she does enjoy the routine and stability of working regularly outside of the home, and how having a job outside of the home personally and socially widens her own horizons. Su can also say that she is the sole financial provider for her family, and self-mastery lends itself to self-confidence and personal pride.

The next vocational transition that Su anticipates would be a parallel position at her job, as she is still under union contract and protection, and isn't interested in a move to management (one level above her current supervisory role). "I am already thinking about what life will look like after retirement, and I regularly put money into a deferred compensation account (which is retirement money above and beyond my expected pension)."

Su Logan's advice to anyone going back into the workforce during a separation or divorce "is to find a neutral advocate who can advise you in financial and legal matters, to handle your stress day-by-day, and don't be afraid to ask family or friends for additional help when it is needed."

Dr. Elisabeth Kubler-Ross: The Five Stages of Grief

No discussion of grief is complete without a foray into the penultimate work of the most famous "doctor of grief", Dr. Elisabeth Kubler-Ross.

Dr. Elisabeth Kubler-Ross was one of the foremost contemporary observers of grieving, death and dying, and of people who were grieving transitions or traumas. She was a psychiatrist and a self-made sociologist whose curiosity about grief first peaked during her work with terminally ill patients in the 1950's and 60's. She developed this Process for examining, labeling, and working through grief:

The Five Stages of Grief	Elisabeth Kübler-Ross
EKR stage	Interpretation
1 - Denial	Denial is a conscious or unconscious refusal to accept facts, information, reality, etc., relating to

	the situation concerned. It's a defense mechanism and perfectly natural. Some people can become locked in this stage when dealing with a traumatic change that can be ignored. Death of course is not particularly easy to avoid or evade indefinitely.
2 - Anger	Anger can manifest in different ways. People dealing with emotional upset can be angry with themselves, and/or with others, especially those close to them. Knowing this helps keep us detached and non-judgmental when experiencing the anger of someone who is very upset.
3 - Bargaining	Traditionally the bargaining stage for people facing death can involve attempting to bargain with whatever God the person believes in. People facing less serious trauma can bargain or seek to negotiate a compromise. For example "Can we still be friends?.." when facing a break-up. Bargaining rarely provides a sustainable solution, especially if it's a matter of life or death.
4 - Depression	Also referred to as preparatory grieving. In a way it's the dress rehearsal or the practice run for the 'aftermath' although this stage means different things depending on whom it involves. It's a sort of acceptance with emotional attachment. It's natural to feel sadness and regret, fear, uncertainty, etc. It shows that the person has at least begun to accept the reality.
5 - Acceptance	Again this stage definitely varies according to the person's situation, although broadly it is an indication that there is some emotional detachment and objectivity. People dying can enter this stage a long time before the people they leave behind, who must necessarily pass through their own individual stages of dealing with the grief.

On Death and Dying, 1997, Elisabeth Kubler-Ross, Scribner Publishing.

Dr. Kubler-Ross acknowledged that these stages (which are not linear, but are identifiable and defined) also apply to big life transitions and traumas other than death. If healthy grief is a letting-go of one experience to embrace another, our goal should be to identify how and when vocational grieving has become unhealthy, or has stopped our personal progression. We should also seek to identify and utilize those coping mechanisms that result in positive professional, psychological, and physical consequences.

In the chapters to follow, we'll examine the phases of vocational transition as described in the Personal Transition Curve Process (courtesy of John M. Fisher) via the stories of those who have "been there, done that." John M. Fisher used Dr. Elisabeth Kubler-Ross' Five Stages of Grief in the development of his Process. We will also explore how age, race, gender, family, and cultural differences factor into the ways a person copes throughout the Personal Transition Curve.

We will use J.M. Fisher's Process to reflect upon which stage each person seems to be experiencing, but will also see whether <u>what</u> compelled the transition affects how they respond to changes in jobs, identities, and circumstances.

Chapter 3:
First Careers: Finding Your Path

    The first significant vocational transition that many people experience is the transition between high school or university and their first "real" job. Especially in America, teenagers and young adults tend to work a succession of minimum wage, minimum requirement jobs before achieving an associate's or bachelor's degree, and typically work their first full-time job in the months after university. For the first time, the crushing responsibility and pressure of making 'something' of oneself is most real. The prospect of failing at this endeavor and having to return to one's family of origin for assistance seems to be impetus enough to push through any personal or professional reservations in a first career (Smith, 2013). And with America holding the distinction of having the most expensive system of higher education in the world, this country's student loan debt means that more matriculated students are likely to move back in with family members to afford other living expenses (Sheehy, 2013). The pressure on first career workers is considerable, albeit normative. How does a first career worker make decisions about what career to pursue, where to live, how to shape their own destiny? The following people all answer those questions very differently, and we will see that their decisions were influenced by culture, family, opportunity, or even fate.

Katie Doyle: Her Love Of People Created A Divergent Path

Katie Doyle is a bright, vivacious 25-year-old woman with a tendency to gently banter during conversation. We meet in her "garden apartment" (an apartment that you walk down into from the street, whose windows are close to or level with the sidewalk). It's within short walking distance from two or three university campuses in Pittsburgh's Oakland neighborhood, and the building is very old and sturdy. It's the apartment you would imagine an English major residing in: small, warm, neat and homey, decorated with classic scarves and books, candles and artistic prints.

Most college graduates who earn their bachelor's degree in English Literature end up either going forward to achieve their master's, or getting a certification so that they can teach English in high school. But Katie Doyle had already enjoyed volunteering in an interdenominational campus ministry group (University Christian Outreach, or U.C.O.) while studying at the University of Pittsburgh. "I decided to take a year off from educational or career development to fully enter the field of pastoral work with Christian women, and did so by networking with my contacts at Michigan State's U.C.O." She began a position on the campus of Michigan State while in the Happiness stage of Fisher's Process.

Katie decided to work a mission year as a household leader for a group of women who shared a house in Lansing, Michigan. "My 'job' was to facilitate a shared life atmosphere, to assist the women with cooperative living, to facilitate personal spiritual development through prayer times and shared meals, and to mediate any personal or functional disputes when necessary." She also encouraged the women to participate in denominational services and weekly U.C.O. meetings.

Although Katie has two sisters, she wasn't completely prepared for the relational and functional complexity that arises from five women sharing a home. There was no shared familial history to work from, no shared personal history to use as a foundation, so "I did my best to help the women to develop warm and trusting relationships with each other. It really was a complex equation; some of the women were more defensive, or didn't trust other women (maybe because of hurt feelings developed by past friendships)." There was a guardedness in the dynamics of the house that was baffling at times, since the household could have been a fresh start. This complexity caused Katie to move into (and through) the Fear/Threat/Guilt stages of Fisher's Process:

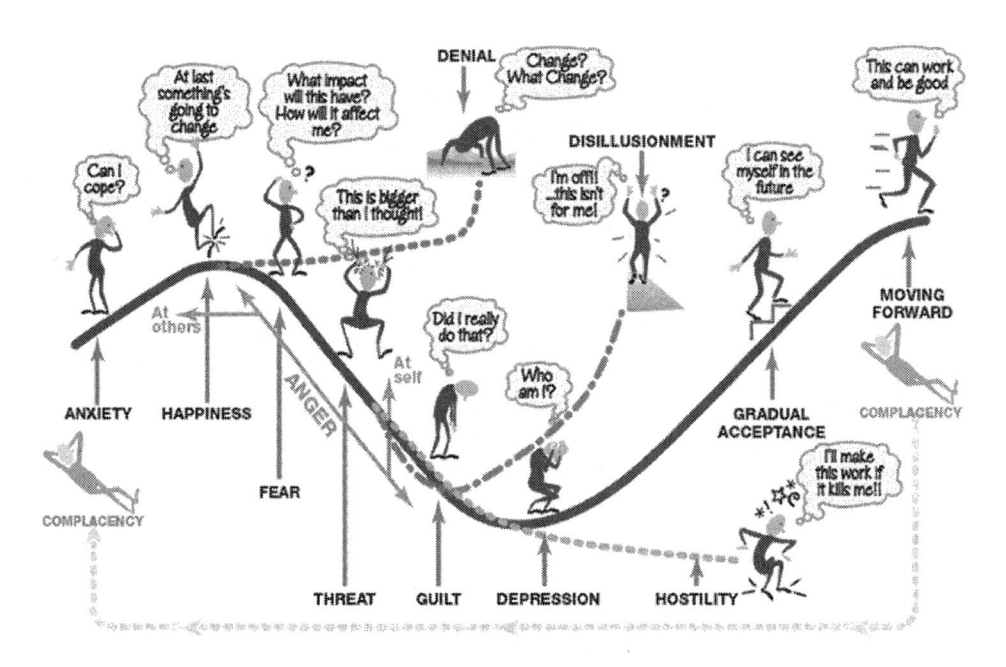

And under work/mission pressures, Katie had to develop new coping and facilitating skills to keep the household functioning and moving forward in a positive direction.

That year of household leadership also helped Katie to develop some new pastoral and teambuilding skills. She was responsible for a small group, assisting in evangelistic outreach activities with the campus ministry, and investing in personal relationships with the other members of the campus ministry team. This new experience helped Katie to develop a confidence in taking initiative.

It also helped her to realize that human endeavors are unpredictable and messy, but glorious. "There were lots of complicated interpersonal issues that came up that year, that the small group leaders had to support each other through while still maintaining the confidence of the students. That year helped me to see that, at least for the foreseeable future, I want to make a vocation from working with and serving college students."

Katie returned to Pittsburgh after the year in Michigan, and spent the next year facilitating a shared campus ministry women's household in the city. Some of the new household members already had pre-existing friendships and relationships through campus ministry involvement or mission trips, which was good. Compared to the household in Michigan, though, Katie felt a distinct difference in her role: "I felt somewhat isolated from the larger group because I had a more hierarchical role in leadership, and there was also a change in campus ministry leadership that affected the dynamics of the social interactions of the group." Katie and two other campus ministry team members shared leadership in the new team, so that put Katie in a leadership role in two spheres of the women's household members' lives. However, Katie had the flexibility, coping skills, and determination to move her into the Gradual Acceptance stage.

Facing these new challenges created an opportunity for change in Katie's life: "I spent my walks to campus in total silence, wrestling with myself. I also went to church services during the day, during the week, usually four times a week. That time with myself and with God helped me to develop feelings of generosity and mercy towards the household members. The time alone helped me to see how complex and beautiful people are, to think about why someone is the way that they are, what are their values? What are their needs?"

The second household leadership year also helped Katie to develop more mediation skills, which forced her to be more analytical in her role. She started to see that her normative response to rigid roles or values was to respond with extreme flexibility by doing things for others, such as hospitality. Katie reflected these findings to her mother (who was in a coordinating role for the women's household) and to the Household Supervisor. Katie learned that she shouldn't settle for less, but also how she could make the best of a difficult situation, and that support helped to transition her into the Moving Forward stage.

After that year (2012-13), Katie experienced some relational shifts and losses of friendships that further cemented the idea that people constantly change and move on, and that Katie would just have to adjust to the tides of change that were outside of her control. "I rely more on God and have a much better prayer life now that I am depending on Him alone, so although I miss my friends, I know that I can do things that He has asked me to do." Additionally, Katie has a special friendship with her mother, and her whole family is very supportive of her missionary role on campus. Katie receives valuable prayer and practical support from the members of her prayer community, as they support her work in U.C.O. The atmosphere and culture in U.C.O. and in her prayer community are a very positive aspect of her life in ministry. She receives encouragement, validation in her role, and prayer support from her pastoral worker (small group leader) and from her supervisor who keeps in regular contact.

"These two valuable years of household experience helped prepare me for the leadership role that I am currently in": a paid position in the University Christian Outreach at the University of Pittsburgh, a vocation she plans to stay in for the foreseeable future. Katie especially appreciates that those two significant experiences have helped her to see that "people are people and NOT products. They are messy, unpredictable, and lovely. I started to see that generosity and mercy can come from difficult circumstances and situations."

Katie's advice to others at vocational crossroads is this: "Don't make fear-based decisions because of the economy or the job market; the world needs us to make people-making decisions based on your passions and what God wants you to do! Think outside of the box; do things that will grow you as a person, even if those things might make you a little uncomfortable."

Poyung Lin: Compelled by National Pride and Personal Drive

I meet with Poyung Lin on campus, in a ubiquitous coffee shop bustling with disheveled, intense and fast-talking university students. His intense gaze and guarded economy of language initially make it difficult for me to engage Poyung, but once he understands that I expect him to tell his own story in his own words, he relaxes. His tall frame leans back, his hands fall open, and he begins:

As a citizen of Taiwan, for Poyung Lin, the impetus for vocational change came from the realization at university that Taiwan's trade cooperation with China was crucial to Taiwan's global survival. To that end, Poyung knew that he needed real professional training and knowledge so that he could help to teach his country's business professionals to compete (and trade) with China on a global level. By fall of 2013, he had graduated from Cheng Kung University in Taiwan with a bachelor's degree dual major in History and Politics, and his master's degree in International Relations from the National Taiwan

University in Taipei. "But I still felt that something was missing from my understanding of global markets and competition, so I applied to universities in the United States and was accepted to the University of Pittsburgh for the master's program in International Relations," says Poyung, age 28. He was in the Disillusionment Phase of Fisher's Process: he realized that a change was coming, and decided to be the orchestrator of change, instead of a reactor TO change.

The road to university status and acceptance in the United States is not easy; Poyung devoted one whole year to the process. For six months he prepared to take the immigration tests, including English proficiency; and for another six months, he studied for the University of Pittsburgh admission requirements, including the G.R.E. (Graduate Record Examinations) and T.O.E.F.L. (Test of English as a Foreign Language). He also traveled to the United States in March of 2014 to tour several universities, including Penn State University and the University of Pittsburgh.

Poyung then returned to Asia and took a 15-day tour through Xunan, China to focus himself for the path ahead of him. "I needed to listen to my inner voice; but how could I hear my inner voice with all of the noise in my everyday life?" He met many interesting people, including a man from Spain who didn't speak English, but did speak Taiwanese. This man had spent ten years backpacking all over the world: "he lived very simply, like a Buddhist monk. He told me to be prepared for everything, including death." Poyung thoroughly enjoyed his "unplugged" experience in China, and paid attention to what the locals talked about: "The people there didn't care about money, but they were very concerned about the environment and the world around them."

In August of 2014, Poyung moved to the United States and began his government-sponsored master's program at the University of Pittsburgh. From all his descriptions, he is now firmly in the Depression stage of Fisher's Process: "I am still adjusting to life here. I still wake up and automatically think in Taiwanese. I miss my country, the food, the language, all the things I have in common with my fellow man. I feel very nostalgic, which is to me both mental and emotional. I talk to my parents twice a week, they miss me and my sister very much." Poyung's only sibling is his sister, who lives in Seattle and is working on her Ph.D. Poyung's parents willingly supported and encouraged their children to attend university in the United States, knowing that their increase in experience and knowledge would eventually benefit Taiwan. "At first, I wanted to be a statesman or politician in Taiwan, but I eventually realized that there is more change that you can create by being a university professor and teaching people. That's why I know that I need to go on and get my Ph.D., so that I can go home, teach business owners how to compete globally, and change Taiwan for the better from the inside."

Poyung's ideals keep him focused on the future, not only his own, but on his country's future. He is in a constant state of Moving Forward, a stage of Fisher's Process that involves experimenting with one's own environment in an active and effective way. By acting in line with one's convictions, beliefs and values, one is always making 'the right choice'.

Poyung's experience of Taiwan is that his own generation is very suspicious of the Chinese government and Communism, and don't know how to relate to China on a global business level. But to Poyung, China represents a deep, proud culture; a thriving government; and global business leadership and acumen. Poyung wants Taiwan to remain independent from China, but he wishes his country would learn how to cooperate with China in business ventures and projects. "I believe that you can import and export to a country, without being owned by them. I want to help Taiwan to make the right choice about China by getting educated about it."

Poyung will spend the summer and fall of 2015 applying to Ph.D. programs in England, including Cambridge and Oxford. His second-level choice would be Princeton or Harvard, here in the States. If he is not accepted into a doctorate program, he will return to Taiwan and work as an international relations analyst or a reporter. Poyung knows that it is a whole separate immigration process to go to university in Europe, which is why he plans to start the process a year before his projected master's graduation date of April 2016.

Poyung fends off his homesickness for Taiwan by cooking traditional dishes at home, by socializing primarily with students who are here from his home country, and by always speaking Taiwanese with friends. Poyung has no desire to take on American social or political values, and regularly contacts his mentor in Taiwan, who shares with Poyung concerns about Taiwan's economic and business future. Poyung's mentor is a university professor in Taipei who wanted Poyung to get his doctorate in his home country: "He encourages me but wants me to come back to Taiwan," but Poyung admits, "I gave up so much to come here!" Regarding the decision to leave his homeland,

Poyung is moving towards the Gradual Acceptance stage of Fisher's Transition Process: he is at the start of managing control over the changes he has made in his life to achieve this educational and professional goal. He is making sense of the "what" and "why" of his decision, and is experiencing an increasing level of self-confidence. He feels good that he has done the right things in the right away, regardless of the sacrifices made.

Poyung left behind his parents in Taiwan, as well as a thriving social and intellectual community, and a serious girlfriend. "Breaking up with her was so difficult to do, but I had to do it. A clean break was best. She was very much in support of what I am trying to do, but we couldn't stay together." Poyung regularly phones his parents and his sister in Seattle, and Matt, a friend that he made during his visit to Penn State in March of 2014. "They have a lot of confidence in me and are very encouraging." He also left behind familiar cultural and social expectations: "Americans are less conservative than Taiwanese, and they always expect to shake hands. Also, I have experienced racism here, especially from homeless people who are confrontational, and pursue me and my friends after we tell them we don't have money. So, I follow the advice of one of my friends, which is just to keep walking." Poyung articulates that he needs more time to feel at home here; he knows that he needs to expand his social networks a little more, but going to classes and studying means that he only sleeps for six to eight hours per night, "so when would I fit in more social time?"

Poyung's advice for others who are considering a similar vocational decision? "FOLLOW YOUR HEART. Don't stay in a job that you don't like, be brave, just take your stuff and go!"

FongZhan Tsai: Higher Learning and Lofty Goals

Meeting FongZhan Tsai for the first time in a coffee shop in the Pittsburgh's Oakland neighborhood, I am first concerned that I might not be able to understand FongZhan in such a loud place. After all, English is his second (or third!) language, and I have no experience with Taiwanese. So, I engage him in casual conversation for ten minutes or so, and become quickly captivated by two aspects of FongZhan's personality: his animated communication style, and his wonderment at all things American. FongZhan's body exudes a quick energy, he often talks with his hands while expounding on a thought, and the more coffee he drinks, the faster he talks. It becomes apparent that FongZhan has fallen in love with America, and of those things he does not understand, he is actively seeking knowledge. He also seems eager to explain why he would choose to leave his native language, culture, land, and family behind.

For FongZhan, five years working in physical therapy in Taiwan had taught him many things, most of all how to treat patients in the least amount of time. FongZhan was expected to "treat" forty to sixty patients per shift, mostly by identifying pain centers on clients' bodies and treating those areas with electrical stimulation and heating pads. There was no time allowable to teach patients about how to prevent further injury, nor how to strengthen the injured areas when they returned home.

"State-sponsored healthcare limits in Taiwan set laws for the treatment of clinic patients, and they say that they should be treated for a full hour; but most clinics have these under-the-table rules, that you are treating at least four patients per hour. You are physically treating one patient as three others are on exercise bikes, and that is included in the treatment time." After five years of experiencing professional frustration and burnout, FongZhan found himself in the Disillusionment stage of Fisher's Process; he became aware that his own values and goals for his profession were incompatible with those of physical therapy care in Taiwan, and wanted to do something about it.

Through the physical therapists' grapevine, FongZhan discovered that various American universities offered master's degrees in physical therapy, and so he started researching how to leave Taiwan and continue in higher education in the United States. "I am 31 years old now, and had a choice: I could stay home and remain in a profession that didn't really help patients, or I could leave everything I knew and come here for a better life and more possibilities."

In March of 2013, FongZhan began his journey by finding the proficiency tests that are required to be accepted at American universities, including the University of Pittsburgh, where he was ultimately accepted. The appeal of coming to the United States started growing as he discovered that the University of Pittsburgh trained graduate students in the newest physical therapy techniques and technology. His research also uncovered that physical therapists in the U.S. are treated like medical professionals and have a satisfying work environment. "It was a little bit intimidating to think about what I had to do to leave Taiwan, but I just took everything step by step. I studied for the English proficiency tests (there are two), I applied for graduate programs, I took the proficiency tests, and collected recommendation letters. I applied at three different graduate schools, worked until May 2014, and then came here in July of that year." FongZhan had reached the stage of Happiness in Fisher's Process, which is both an acceptance of inevitable change, and an impetus to make the change happen.

As a single man, FongZhan's ties to Taiwan rested solely on his family. "My parents were very supportive. My parents are very proud of me, and gave me the money to come here. I also saved a lot of money in the year I was getting prepared to come to America. I have a brother and sister who live close to my parents, and three nieces and two nephews. I miss them very much, I call them and talk to them whenever I can, but I am so busy with school that I don't even have time to work a job while I am doing this program. I also have a couple of close friends that I miss, but I probably won't see them again unless I go home to see my family."

There are people here in America who made FongZhan's transition to his new life much easier. He has a close Taiwanese friend whom he socializes with who attends the same university. A Christian group on campus, called U.C.O. (University Christian Outreach) have also become his new support, and he considers many of them to be his friends. He does activities with the group, spends time with them on the weekends, and has been invited to share American holidays with them. He especially values those experiences, as his goal is to experience as much American life as possible: the food, the language, the interaction, the humor, even the dating. "Americans are much more conversational than in Taiwan; there is more talking and much more hugging."

The American openness and friendliness that FongZhan regularly encounters has been key to positioning him in the Moving Forward stage of Fisher's Process. He is comfortable with his decision to come to the United States to pursue higher education, and has seen mostly positive results from the decision to leave his family, country, and culture behind. Sometimes, though, the cultural differences can be overwhelming and confusing. One time he was in a local bar and was spontaneously kissed by a very forward-thinking woman: "I just couldn't believe it! I didn't even know her! It was - how would you say? - strange and AWKWARD."

FongZhan has also experienced multiple incidents of racism, both when alone and when with friends. He tries not to take it personally, but stays aware, so he doesn't get in situations that might turn into violent encounters. He has one very good friend who insists that they speak in their native language (Taiwanese), though FongZhan would prefer to always speak in English, "which supports my future plans to stay permanently in the United States, and socially, makes belonging easier." From these accommodations that he is making, it is obvious that he is deciding on staying in America.

One of the most impactful, unforeseen complications of FongZhan's graduate program at the University of Pittsburgh is that there aren't any other Taiwanese students in his classroom work group, which gives him no options for study partners. "The whole class, except for me, has options for studying. The class is made up of Indians, Nigerians, and Saudi Arabians. And then there is me," he says with a grin. The language barrier was so great when he first started the program, that he recorded each class lecture to play it back slowly during his study time, so that he could take accurate notes for studying later. The teacher's assistant that lead the recitation classes also had "a very heavy Indian accent, so that was an additional difficulty." FongZhan handled these barriers with an approach that has served him most well in his transition to American life: "Be tough but flexible. Prepare yourself for mental 'construction' when doing something so new. And get used to feeling lonely."

FongZhan plans is to graduate with his Masters in Physical Therapy (MSPT) in August of 2015, to study for a month or so, and to take the certification exam in October. If he does not pass his exam, he will pursue a full-time position in a physical therapy practice and try the exam some other time. "I really get enjoyment out of treating people and teaching them the mind/body connection. I believe in using humor, sympathy and compassion to help a person to heal. Most especially, the stroke patients that I worked with in Taiwan benefited from that." The other consideration is that Pennsylvania law is for a non-citizen to work and live in one other state for at least a year, before settling down in this state. "I love Pittsburgh, but can't stay here after graduation, so I am considering New York or Ohio, so that I can go to the tennis tournaments there." Tennis is one of FongZhan's favorite activities, and keeps him trim and fit for all the challenges of his life.

FongZhan's advice to anyone experiencing such a drastic vocational and geographical shift is to be independent, to find a way to make the situation work for themselves. "Record your classes, so that you can be successful and also learn better English. Find an organization like U.C.O. so that you can have a group of people who can make you feel at home and relaxed. Spend a lot of time with people who will speak English with you, and show you American food."

Sandra Cahalan: Type A Personality turned Campus Missionary

Sandra Cahalan (Sandy) and I meet in May of 2016 on the spacious front porch of her parents' brick home, in a small western suburb of Pittsburgh. Sandy and I have known each other a long time. I used to babysit her and her siblings when they were children, and our families are members of a local Christian group. Sandy is a little taller than me with white-blonde hair, translucent skin, bright eyes and stylish clothes. She perches on the edge of the couch, attentive and engaged.

In the summer of 2014, Sandy was getting ready to enter her senior year of college at the University of Pittsburgh. Everything was on track for after graduation and her plans were set: she had taken her GREs (Graduate Record Examinations) with the goal of attending graduate school for Speech Pathology after completing her bachelors in Communication Sciences & Disorders, she was in a serious relationship with a young man, and everything was going smoothly. "But suddenly, our relationship ended, which made me question everything else in my life. I am a Type A person. I like to make a plan, follow it closely, and finish strong. I like to have control and am very organized. What happens when that gets derailed? Because I am a Christian, I felt very strongly that I should take some time, regroup, and pray about what to do next."

While praying, Sandy felt very strongly that God was asking her to give up her grad school plans (at least temporarily); although this meant that yet another part of her life had taken an unexpected turn, Sandy was very much at peace. Normally when things happened that didn't fit into her 5-Year Plan, Sandy felt anxious and sometimes got testy with people, but not in this situation. She consulted with her friend Stephanie regarding her sense about putting off grad school, and sought her advice. Stephanie suggested that Sandy might want to consider a mission year through Kairos, a Christian organization that helps to facilitate mission work for college age Christians.

Sandy discussed this option with her parents, who were supportive but also had practical concerns about Sandy taking time off before starting graduate school. They knew that Sandy would be responsible to raise funds to finance her mission year, and she was amid a very busy senior year of college. Nonetheless, her parents were very supportive of her plans going forward and knew that Sandy had devoted time, consideration, and discussion before going forward.

"I completed the online application for a mission year in December of 2014, and had an interview with Kairos' Mission Director in February of 2015. By March I had been accepted into the Mission program and was given a choice about where I would be placed in university campus missions. Because the University Christian Outreach (U.C.O.) in Maryland had no female mission leader yet, I chose that location. In the meantime, I carried on with my senior year at Pitt, which was very busy. But I had a lot of support from Stephanie and other friends, and also my parents. They were very reassuring and affirmed me, and also prayed for me during that time. They really wanted me to be firm in my commitment, but also comfortable with the decision."

Sandy graduated from the University of Pittsburgh in April of 2015, and committed herself to a year of U.C.O. mission work in Adelphi, Maryland. Sandy met with other women who had served as U.C.O. staff in Pittsburgh, which gave her some insight as to what to expect from her mission year. They gave her good advice on what to expect from the job, how to establish healthy boundaries with the students in U.C.O., student vs staff boundaries, and they developed authentic friendships with Sandy through this process. Sandy also depended upon her friendship with two of her siblings, who had similar experiences with university mission work, which is evangelism as a full-time job.

"I got in contact with other young people from Maryland's U.C.O. chapter, and attended a fundraising "boot camp" in May in Ypsilanti, Michigan which was sponsored by Kairos. At the boot camp I made friends with Jerel, who is another UCO staff person on the Maryland campus. I was assigned a fundraising mentor, who gave me some creative ideas on how to raise the funds I needed for the following year, in just 100 days of summer." By the first week of August, Sandy was packing up her belongings and moving to Maryland. She moved into a house with three other female UCO staff, all either part time paid or volunteer workers.

"It was a whirlwind time; the following week, I traveled to Lansing, Michigan to attend a staff training for three days (I still have trainings there, two times each semester). I met other UCO staff at that training, and received a lot of encouragement and advice for the semester to come. That same month I traveled to Lawton, Michigan for Summer Academy, which is structured training on how to evangelize. We were trained on guided personal prayer, Catholic and Protestant theology, and did real-world evangelization in the surrounding area." By the end of August, Sandy's schedule had really ramped up, including the university's Freshman Fair. The Fair was segregated into subjects, such as Greek Life, academic clubs, volunteer opportunities, and clubs (sports, religious, and the arts). Sandy met incoming freshmen, introduced them to U.C.O. life, explained the U.C.O. mission, and collected their contact information. She organized weekly U.C.O. group meetings, helped them to form small groups and assigned small group leaders, facilitated social gatherings for the group, encouraged each student in their educational and spiritual lives, and performed countless administrative tasks associated with her role.

Sandy also began attending bi-weekly prayer meetings with a local ecumenical Christian community that financially supports Maryland's U.C.O. chapter. "My women's group has been a real support for me, and the group leader is one of my mentors. It is a respite for me, to go to prayer meetings and to my small group. UCO work can be very draining, but community life helps to fill me back up for the following week." The one experience that was not as positive, was that her ex-boyfriend moved into the area for his job, and joined the same community. Eventually, Sandy came to see that contact with him in that environment helped her to resolve any "dangling threads" of resentment or hurt that were created by their breakup.

Sandy really enjoys her position as UCO mission leader, so much that she decided to sign up for a second mission year on the same university campus. "Our campus has a very urban setting, so I am constantly socializing with a very multicultural group of people. My own white privilege has come into focus for me, and I have become more aware of my own limited experiences and upbringing. I have become more open to new music, new cultures, and new people! This experience has really expanded my perspective on the world. I have registered as a resident of Maryland, officially joined the community here, and for now, this is my home." Sandy is very busy now, but is still aware that her long-term future is unsure. Depending on how the second year of mission work goes, she has some other decisions she needs to keep in mind: "If I feel that I am going to get married and have kids, does it make sense for me to go to graduate school? I am now paying for my bachelor's degree, and graduate school is very expensive. Although I have applied to grad schools, I am also considering taking the Praxis Exams, which is the first step towards certification for public school teaching. I already know that I prefer early childhood stages of teaching, which would allow me to facilitate early intervention for kids with speech delays and disorders. For now, my next vocational stage is really up in the air, but I am still planning for several different avenues of progress."

Sandy's advice is to lean into the support that you already have, and to seek it out if you don't have it: "If you don't have a mentor in your intended field, find one!" She has discovered that establishing a regular prayer and meditation time, and guarding that time carefully, can help to center and calm herself, and creates positivity. "The risk of taking a completely different path is worth it! Despite the struggles and anxiety, I am right where I am supposed to be. Two things that have also helped are journaling and having a 'passion planner', which has guided questions so that I can look back after a month and see how things went. Being able to see your progress on paper is a real validation and encouragement for when things get difficult."

Haya Eason: The City and Color

I meet with Haya Eason in her house, a mid-sized home in the South Hills of Pittsburgh, about 35 minutes from downtown. She introduces me to her teenage daughter and her husband, offers me something to drink, and then we settle at her dining room table. Haya is neatly dressed in professional clothing, having just come home from work, and her posture is straight-backed but open, with her shoulders back and her chin up, typical military body language.

"I was just past my 18th birthday when I joined the Marines with my boyfriend, who was looking for a way out of Detroit's West Side": this is Haya Eason's explanation of how her military career began. Haya's mother was, understandably, very upset with the decision, probably even more so when Haya's boyfriend was discharged from the military after he got injured during boot camp. But Haya had made a commitment, and she was determined to go through with it.

Haya's adjustment to military life was rough: "I admit, I had a chip on my shoulder about authority, and I had a tough time being in a situation where people were constantly telling me what to do." Going from the rough, independent atmosphere of urban Detroit to the highly structured, interdependent atmosphere of the Marines (traditionally a male-dominated branch of the U.S. military) was incredibly difficult. Over time, Haya learned when to fall back - and when to fight for her place in the Marines. And as an African-American woman, she learned that she had to define for herself what that "place" was.

Several incidents happened that made it harder to find her place, though; one was the rape of a fellow female Marine by a male Marine that was - alarmingly - covered up by the military, and then there were multiple incidents of racism that Haya personally experienced that made her skeptical of the military's ability to protect her work environment. "However, I did have several allies, including the Chief Warrant Officer, who helped me to negotiate the processes of filing complaints and getting the incidents documented or resolved."

After 6 years as a Discharge Clerk in the Marines, Haya received her "B Billet," which is a short-term assignment to another duty (or job description), which she fulfilled in Japan for a year and eight months, and then she was honorably discharged. She spent her B Billet time in Japan getting her finances in order, and trying to mentally disentangle herself from the military identity that she had been entrenched in for so long. She was in the Disillusionment and Denial phases of Fisher's Process: she knew she was unhappy and wanted to leave the military, but didn't know what her life could look like outside of it. It wasn't that she wasn't ready to leave the military, but leaving her military family behind would be difficult. For some time, she continued to attend various on-base social activities: "I tried to hang on to base life longer than I should have; I was grieving that I wasn't a Marine anymore, and didn't have anyone in my family to seek advice from, to know how to do that well," she says. Once Haya began to transition out of the military, she experienced the Depression phase of Fisher's Process. She still had several military friends whom she had bonded with, and they were supportive; but they were still active in the military and couldn't sympathize with the process of transition that she was experiencing.

Haya received spiritual direction and advice during her transition to civilian life from a friend in her barracks in Japan, with whom she had been attending church services and Bible studies. Haya saw the church services as a break from her all-encompassing military life; the church was off the military base, and had few military members. The members of her church were her emotional and spiritual support during her transition from military life, while she was still overseas. While praying one day about whether she should leave military life, she very clearly felt that she was hearing God tell her, "it's okay for you to go now," and that helped her to solidify her decision to permanently separate from the Marines. Haya had moved into the Gradual Acceptance phase of Fisher's Process.

Haya returned to America, and settled in Charleston, South Carolina. She worked for Kelly Girl Services for a short time (during which she again moved into the Disillusionment phase), then procured a position with the City of Charleston: "I realized that I worked better in highly structured jobs that had a lower level of office politics." She began in the Building Inspection Department, and she stayed in that job for almost six years, during which time she experienced the Moving Forward phase. She was in Charleston for eight years, from 1990 to 1998; moved to North Carolina for a job in 1998 and stayed there until 2001; and then moved to Pittsburgh that year after she married her husband, one of her best friends and supports.

One of the things that made it easier to separate from the military was Haya's observation that most women in the Marines had advanced in their careers by sleeping their way up the ranks, which she refused to do. If she were to advance, she wanted to know that it was based on her own merits. She also experienced (in the first six years that she lived on base in the American South) blatant racism, some of it institutional and ignored or tolerated by her superiors, some of it more social and subtle. Having to live her life according to Christian principles was very difficult in these situations, since the human side of her was so angry that racism would be tolerated within "the brightest and the best," the U.S. Marines.

Being in the military helped Haya to see where her personal worth and values were; what field she wanted to end up in (social services); and how to prioritize her vocational values. Haya, age 51, now works part-time doing what she loves, working directly with - and on behalf of - people. She has a teenage daughter with her husband, and a mother who is in a nursing home in a local community so that Haya can advocate for her and visit her often. "I would love to go to college and earn my Bachelor's, but the timing isn't right yet; maybe college is for when my daughter is a bit older and needs me less?"

Julia Chun Hee Hong: I Am Just A Visitor Here

"Julia" Chun Hee Hong is a vibrant, diminutive woman from South Korea who both shakes my hand upon the moment of introduction - and slightly bows her head. In many Asian cultures, it is considered rude, aggressive, or controversial to look a person in the eye, especially upon initial introduction. Having had a Japanese roommate, Hiromi, who taught me some of the cultural expectations of majority-Asian cultures, I knew this already, and that it would have been rude for me to attempt to strongly catch Julia's eye at any point, especially considering the common rules for social etiquette (Bosrock,1994), and the cultural differences in how a young person treats a person of their own generation vs an older cohort (they are not considered social equals). There are several stops and starts to the beginning of our meeting, until Julia is familiar with what I am asking of her (nothing too personal), and how long our meeting will last. The coffee shop on the east end of the Oakland neighborhood of Pittsburgh is teeming with life and noise, and we find a quieter corner in which to talk. This is an important thing to do, both for clarity's sake (Julia is not fully fluent in English), and for ambiance (nothing is more distracting/tempting than a barista yelling scrumptious- sounding, complicated coffee orders - at least for myself). We settle into the corner, and begin.

"Julia is not my real name, I adopted that name after repeating my real name, Hee Hong, over again many times, when I first moved to the United States. It is easier for people to understand and to remember!" According to Julia, many of her Korean friends have also adopted American first names to fit in, and for efficiency. It is particularly problematic to use Korean protocol for names in America, because Americans do not know the proper order for Korean names. For example: Julia's family name is Chun (what other cultures describe as a "last name"); her shared given name is Hee (her mother's "maiden name"); and her given name is Hong (her "first name"). In addressing Julia according to Korean social etiquette, she would be addressed as Hee Hong or Ms. Chun (dependent upon person who is talking to Julia at any point). "Within a work environment in South Korea, I would be addressed by my work title, not my given name." Work titles serve to keep a workplace's hierarchy in place, and everyone knows the company hierarchy's 'pecking order' by the title with which each person is addressed (Bosrock, 1994).

What compelled Julia to come to America for a master's degree was simple: in South Korea, it is very difficult to work in Occupational Therapy and make enough income to live independently. One of her professors at her undergraduate university (Far East University in

Gyeonggi-do, South Korea), encouraged Julia to consider a master's degree in Occupational Therapy (O.T.) in America and then maybe a research position at a university here. Julia (age 24) extensively researched student visa requirements for a few years, including English fluency, pre-requirements for applying to university, and what the financial cost would be. During this time of preparation, she began to experience some of the beginning stages of Fisher's Process of the Process of Transition: Anxiety, Happiness and Fear. "I knew that a change was necessary, but also that many big risks and chances came along with my plan."

To begin, Julia traveled to several American universities that were offering master's programs in O.T., including Utah State University, Stanford, and the University of Pittsburgh (where she achieved her master's degree in Occupational Therapy in April of 2015). "I then took English proficiency tests (passing them on the fifth try!), and I also continued with my college studies at Far East University. I also needed three letters of recommendation." Along this personal path to educational and vocational improvements, her parents were her primary financial and emotional supporters. They consistently encouraged her, and despite their own work obligations, made time to listen to her and to help her, in any way possible. Her university professor was also an emotional support, and mentored and cheered her on during this uncertain time. Unfortunately, many of her university friends in South Korea were detrimental to her confidence about the plan to go to America, "because they just didn't believe in my ability to do it."

Julia's preparations for emigration were complicated when she broke her leg after slipping on ice after her graduation from Far East University. Julia had to stay at home for 5 months afterwards, to fully recuperate and regain her health for the trip to the United States.

After fulfilling the many student visa requirements and being accepted to the University of Pittsburgh, Julia moved to Pittsburgh in August of 2014. She had a friend from South Korea who was already in Pittsburgh, who helped her to adjust to American university life. She became involved with a Christian Korean church in Oakland, called The Central Church of Pittsburgh. The church helped Julia to make many new friends (mostly women), and to find a place to fit into, right away. "I experienced a spiritual awakening there. Before I joined Central, I used to just love God, but my life was all about performance, grades, success and money! Now I try to devote every day and all of my things and actions to God." In her monthly phone calls home, Julia can talk to her mother about her spiritual awakenings, maturing and questions. She talks to her father about other things, her classes, her plans and her career aspirations. Julia heard from her mother that her father still goes to work, but is considered semi-retired at work, that he has less authority now because his company was bought by another corporation. "I talk to my mother about all of the personal things, to my father about the professional things and some personal things."

Julia also received assistance in her language transition via five months of English tutoring at the Central Church of Pittsburgh. The language barrier has been particularly difficult, especially since it has created a wall between her and full access to her studies: "I got many personal, individual times of attention from my professor in South Korea. Here, I have not received any personal attention at the University of Pittsburgh, not even when I have emailed them for help. I was very upset by that! It made me feel like they see me as money, not as a student, not as a person." This lack of support made Julia experience a temporary occurrence of the Depression Phase of Fisher's Process: "What have I done?". Because Julia had such a rough start to university life in America, she sought help from the counseling center at Pitt. "I went there as I needed help to be adjusted, but I don't need it now." Julia also received personal attention and friendship from a friend that she had made through the University Christian Outreach at Pitt: "Katie listens to me, she is a very good listener, and she has also helped me to meet other people that I can socialize with." A Korean friend, Sue, has been very supportive of Julia, and has been a lifeline and has helped Julia to maintain her confidence during this difficult time. All of these supports helped to move Julia into the Gradual Acceptance Phase.

Regarding her transition to American university life: "This is not home. New words keep happening in conversation and I have to ask lots of questions. I am not a good cook, and I am not interested in American food, so I eat out a lot, mostly Korean food. I don't feel that I have adjusted." However, Julia has accommodated herself to her surroundings; in other words, the move to America has not been so painful that she has decided when she will definitively return to South Korea. Julia's long range plan is to work for six years as an Occupational Therapist in America, and then apply to a university to earn her doctorate. She plans to then return to South Korea and get married. "I miss my parents, my sister and brother, and all of my high school friends. I hope to be married and return to them someday."

For now, Julia has very little time to date. She gets on a bus at 6:45 each morning, goes to school from 8 am until 5 am, and then returns home by bus. Each day, almost three hours is spent on the bus. Julia uses that time to rest or to study. When she feels stressed, Julia goes with friends to a local cafe, or "I go to the theatre to watch movies, which helps me to escape from my stress. I also spend time with my Taiwanese friend, who has similar holidays to Korea, and we have similar traditions, so that helps me to feel a little closer to home." Julia admits that she still turns down a lot of offers to socialize, "because I have to spend twice as much time studying to understand the content, and I am determined to succeed at school and being in America." Julia promised her parents that she would be successful and thus far, she has certainly done so.

Sometime soon, Julia hopes to secure a full time Occupational Therapy position, and to find a Korean or Korean-American man to marry. She prefers to marry someone who has shared cultural values, "because cultural differences are a big deal, along with the language barrier that I deal with every day." She feels that having a boyfriend or husband would help her to move into the Moving Forward Phase, which is a more permanent state of embracing and finding the good things about her new life.

Julia advises anyone who is about to make a similar decision to think of three very big components to emigration: 1) "If English is not your first language, study conversational English longer! I learned formal English, and that did not help me in conversation. I don't know jargon (slang) very well, and that affects my communication, especially in social situations where lots of people are talking at once." 2) "Do you have confidence in yourself? I mean, a LOT of confidence? You will need it!" and 3) "Do you have a specific and strong desire or reason to leave your home country? Being homesick is a big deal, so you shouldn't leave home just to do something different."

Sarah Nelson: Bridging the Language and Cultural Gap*

"Because cultural differences are a big deal, along with the language barrier that I deal with every day." (Julia Chun Hee Hong)

Since Sarah Nelson* was 15 years old, she felt the intrinsic desire to be an ESL (English as Second Language) Instructor. "And in 11th grade, I attended a college fair and got more information on how exactly I needed to go about it. I decided that I needed to enroll in the English department at a local university, get my bachelor's degree in English along with a teaching certification, but then I also had plans to achieve an ESL Certification. I felt a particular draw towards urban schools with immigrant populations, but that's not where I ended up."

Sarah is a petite, beautiful, and decidedly youthful-looking Caucasian woman. She is full of energy and purpose, and has been very careful about each step in her career, and is a practical person. She is also a prayerful Christian woman who discerns each next step in a considerate way. When Sarah began looking for teaching positions at the end of her last year of university, and found that her high school alma mater offered a significant starting salary and other benefits, she found herself an English teacher and working alongside some of her former high school teachers. The combination of practical considerations and spiritual instinct placed her in a suburban atmosphere, but she soon discovered that an influx of new immigrants to the Pittsburgh suburbs presented a future opportunity to further develop the school system's ESL programs. "Two years after starting as an English teacher, I earned my ESL Certification and then kept an eye on my work environment to see if an opportunity presented itself. In 2014, two years after that, I started working with Spanish-speaking children in the mornings before school. The ESL Instructor for our school was then freed up to work with the Pakistani, Indian, and Vietnamese students. At the end of the 2014-15 school year, that Instructor suddenly retired, and the position was posted via the online bid boards."

Sarah acted quickly; she immediately contacted the school's curriculum director to ask what exactly was involved with the position and the ESL program. "The curriculum director said that the ESL program would need to be completely reorganized, so that the standards of a high-functioning program would be met. I would also have to quickly take the PRAXIS tests to be eligible to run the program, as that would complete my certification to work with children from kindergarten through sixth grade. I immediately registered for the test, and because the test was the next week, didn't have time to properly study for it."

When Sarah's PRAXIS scores came back, they were so good that Sarah took it as a sign to pursue the ESL Instructor position. She talked some more with the curriculum instructor and her boyfriend Brent (now her husband), prayed about it, and decided to move forward. With that decision, she would have to leave behind her team of English teachers, most of whom had become good friends to her. Sarah would also have to give up the SAT prep program and being co-sponsor of the drama club (for which she was able to be part of the costuming crew and fulfill other creative pursuits). Regardless, Sarah interviewed for the position and was accepted, and now would move forward into unfamiliar vocational territory.

Sarah would have to redesign and implement a new ESL program, so that the school would be able to meet the needs of their immigrant students. The 22-year-old program at her school district was not only outdated, but the number of new immigrants in the district was outpacing the capability of one ESL teacher to manage the program. "I realized that getting the program updated would have to include meeting the Pennsylvania Code for ESL Programs. In the beginning stage of instruction, we need to be able to provide two hours of direct daily instruction for each student and then at the middle to high level, one hour per student per day. The only way that one person could satisfy those requirements (and the other responsibilities of the position) would be if we had only six ESL students in our district. By the 2013/14 school year, we had between 15 and 20 identified ESL students. By the 2014/15 school year, we had 30! That number will just go up every year, especially considering global refugee numbers. Chances are, some of the Syrian refugees will end up in our program, and we won't be able to meet the minimum requirement for instruction, nor meet their other needs." The other needs presented for immigrant students include advocacy for the students and their families within the school district, and a higher level of emotional involvement for ESL teachers. ESL students become more dependent on their ESL teachers than other students would, there are language barriers in how students perceive a request or assignment, or personality clashes can get a lesson off-track (Davis, 2016). There can be cross-cultural clashes between individual students, or parents who aren't able to help their children with ESL assignments.

"I knew that I had to become an advocate for the whole ESL Program within the school district. I had to make it clear to school administrators that another full-time teacher had to be added soon, so that we would meet state requirements for instructions, and meet the needs of the children. At minimum, I needed to have seven fully-functioning classes going for kindergarten to 12th grade. I also needed to be able to pre-test each new student, and then test them again in February of each school year, to mark their progress."

At first, Sarah felt like she was drowning, and completely unequipped to meet the needs of her ESL students. She was firmly entrenched in the Fear, Threat and Guilt Stages of Fisher's Process, in which a person realizes that their work choice is much bigger than they initially realized and starts to wonder what kind of impact it will have on their lives. Sarah regularly felt overwhelmed and had second thoughts about the decision - at least in the short-term. She had to give up her curriculum prep periods to add more classes for the children, which meant that she spent a lot of time outside of school preparing her lessons for the different grades, levels, and needs of each child. She also had to work with the complex high school schedule, and then somehow fit instruction for the lower grades between the high school ESL classes. "I saw that the children were not getting their needs met, no matter how well I organized schedules and lesson plans, but I was afraid to ask for another teacher early on." Sarah requested a county teacher's advisor, which the school district had to pay for. Sarah had a monthly individual meeting with the teacher's advisor to get advice on the processes at her job, as the advisor is well-versed on standards that the school districts need to follow. The advisor helped Sarah send her district some reports that showed how the school district was not up to code, which gave her the courage (and backing) to ask for another teacher to be added to the ESL Program.

Along with the support of her teacher's advisor, Sarah's husband Brent provided emotional support and a listening ear. He was very encouraging in all of Sarah's professional efforts, and understood when her work life overlapped onto their relationship and into their personal time. Eventually (especially once the second teacher was added), the new position created a better work/life balance compared to her previous English position, for which she had to take home papers and exams on the weekends. Sarah felt a sense of self-mastery in redesigning the ESL Program, a burgeoning confidence in advocating for her program and her students with the school district, and totally supported by her teacher's advisor and Brent. She knew that she was the best fit for the job, that her compassion for the children and their families would make her a good advocate for them, and that her passion was in helping ESL students smoothly fit into their new schools and to progress in their ESL skills.

As three of the previous interviews have shown, Poyung Lin, Feng-Chan Tsai and Julia Chun all experienced marked difficulties in their functioning in American society due to language barriers. ESL teachers like Sarah can help to bridge the gap for immigrant children and their families, at the very least by showing them that Americans will go above and beyond the call of duty to help them to adjust. Practically, ESL students are given the tools to progress and succeed for as long as they wish to stay here. All that is required is a willing student and a persistent, compassionate teacher. And the United States needs more ESL teachers each year for both children and adults: in 2013, 61.6 million American residents spoke a language other than English at home; 41% of those (approximately 25.1 million) were considered Limited English Proficient: those who speak English less than "very well" (Zong & Batalova, 2015).

Looking back, Sarah says "I should have been more aggressive in making sure another ESL teacher was IMMEDIATELY added. That would have benefitted the students, the program, and myself. I should have followed up with my union regarding the missed prep periods, teachers aren't allowed to be put in situations where they don't have set aside time during the work day in order to achieve their required teaching goals. And, I should have persisted with the administration in making sure that our ESL program was within B.E.C. (Basic Education Circulars). Those laws are put in place to ensure that school districts are following required legislation that ensures that every student gets their educational needs met. When I wanted to push this with the assistant superintendent, he was on leave, and the interim assistant superintendent won't be able to assure our compliance with B.E.C. At first, these kids weren't even getting the legal minimum standards met. It's only since the additional teacher was added that we were meeting standards."

Sarah does miss some benefits to her English teaching position. She has contact with higher numbers of children, between 100 and 200 per year, having a broader reach as a core-class teacher. She also misses the higher level of intellectual discussion with her students that she had in her English classes; her instruction with the ESL students is beginner and rudimentary in comparison. "I also have a gypsy life now; I travel from building to building to teach all of my ESL classes, which means that I have very limited connection to other teachers, the administrator, and the general school culture. I frequently feel disconnected because I float around so much." Sarah says that the ESL students (and their circumstances) are more emotionally demanding than her previous group of students.

The benefits to her ESL position? "I am able to connect cross-culturally with our minority immigrant students. I learn something new, either on a cultural or language level, every day. I have a greater personal impact on these kids, and I get more respect and contact from their parents. Also, personally, I have my weekends back at this point! I easily schedule fun things with Brent or my friends for the weekends, have dinner with friends, and set my work life aside on Saturday and Sunday. I figuratively and literally am able to set work aside when I walk out the door, and don't have to worry about grading papers or tests over the weekend."

Sarah's advice to other teachers facing a similar choice between two good positions? "Getting out of your comfort zone is the harder choice, but totally worth it! When you leave your present position, don't burn bridges; but also, don't let others take advantage of you in your new position. Find a support system that will help you adjust to your new teaching role; whether professional or personal (or both), you need someone to help you at first. Also, be ready to feel inadequate and underprepared at first; that's all normal! Keep a positive attitude and the situation WILL get better. If you are a person of faith, any faith, pray a lot. It will help you to discern when to sit back versus when to push back."

Sarah has been considering what turns she may take in her career. She has become interested in what it would take to become an advocate for her ESL students' parents, how to expand the reach of the school district's ESL program and help it to be a positive force in the community that expands past the physical walls of the school. Sarah is anticipating future connection with one of the adult ESL programs, and to eventually have a full team of ESL teachers within her school's program. So far, these ideas are just brainstorming, mental notes that she makes as she observes gaps in what is needed in the community. But with this ESL teacher - we know that the idea won't stay ephemeral for long.

Ross Acheson: A Shift in Career Discernment

Ross Acheson meets me for dinner in a small Asian restaurant in the Oakland neighborhood of Pittsburgh, his quiet demeanor setting the tone for our interview. He considers carefully each question to ensure that his ideas are coming across in a consistent and coherent manner, his low and measured tone setting a reassuring cadence. "I am interested in telling you how the threads of my spiritual journey have set the scene for my vocational decisions, and for me, that journey really began in junior high."

In eighth grade, Ross Acheson experienced a powerful spiritual conversion that impacted the meaning behind every big life decision going forward. He then became involved with a high school youth group whose members were vibrant Catholic and Protestant Christians; they were all eager to live simply by faith, be involved in mission work, perhaps even consider being clergy. And although Ross had a deep desire to serve God by serving His people, he had not set concrete goals for his educational pursuits. He graduated from high school, settled on Calvin College in Grand Rapids, Michigan, and began his higher education journey.

"I felt ambivalent about the focus of my college life, and felt that academics (in a global sense) were more about the pursuit of truth and grappling with bigger questions of philosophy, theology, and existence." Ross's parents thought that engineering or medical school might best fit him, but at the end of his sophomore year, Ross declared a major in International Development Studies and minors in Religion and Greek. That summer, Ross worked for eight weeks at a children's camp, which included children with special needs. "This experience helped to further cement my desire to serve others and to pursue personal spiritual development. The innocence and curiosity with which they approached their Bible lessons was very refreshing to me!"

It was during his junior year of college that Ross decided to go through a program called R.C.I.A. (Rite of Christian Initiation of Adults) within the Roman Catholic Church. Along with trying to discern his vocational path and working as a Residential Advisor in the dorms, this program and his friends there helped Ross to begin to develop his personal spiritual path in a very concentrated way, which eventually affected his vocational path.

Also, during his junior year, hearing of Ross's past two years of choosing not to date to concentrate on his college studies and spiritual development, his friend from the high school youth group pointed him towards a leader in Detroit Summer Outreach (D.S.O.), a summer missions program working with disadvantaged youth in Detroit, Michigan. The program participants live in a communal atmosphere, live asceticism (very simple lives, without luxury), and learn about urban issues affecting families who live in poverty. They also teach Vacation Bible School lessons to children who participate in the program, and serve in many other ways.

The summer before his senior year in college, as a new Catholic, Ross participated in D.S.O. "That experience served to deplete much of the cynicism that I had experienced as a Calvinist Protestant: it renewed my faith in humanity, refreshed me, and renewed my resolve to live with a passion for living for God. During that summer, I served with members of a celibate layperson brotherhood called Servants of the Word. They are professional men who have taken a vow of celibacy and yet, operate in their jobs, volunteer in their churches and Christian groups, and serve communities. It was very appealing to me, this notion of having a set-aside life though not an ordained priest, deacon, or clergy."

This set-aside life was so appealing to Ross that he became an affiliate member of the brotherhood after he graduated from Calvin College in Grand Rapids, Michigan. That summer, he did another stint in D.S.O. The following fall and winter, he then worked as an inspector in an industrial company, inspecting metal parts and operating a forklift. He enjoyed the job, though it paid low wages; sharing time and stories with men and women of the inner city helped to keep him grounded. Ross also spend a lot of time with the brotherhood, serving and volunteering with a local Christian community.

"The following summer I got a job with a web-based advertising company, getting on-the-job training. That fall I was offered a position with The Servants of the Word (the brotherhood) in Lansing that was split between on-campus mission work (called U.C.O.) and serving the household of the brotherhood. It was a great year! The household was comprised of 4 lifetime committed members and 4 affiliates. We shared meals, prayer times, household work, and other communal activities. I loved it, but my parents were kind of freaked out. They were totally fine with me becoming Catholic and even with me not working a traditional job; but especially my mom thought I should be married and have children. She didn't really understand the point of affiliating with a celibate group of men, and was especially nervous about me considering a lifetime commitment to that group. But my parents' opinions were not a part of the discernment process. I trusted that God would show me the way at each critical juncture. But honestly, even me considering the brotherhood affected my relationship with my parents."

After that year of sharing a house with the Servants of the Word, Ross sensed that his life was going in a different direction. In the following months, Ross was offered three different jobs: a position with D.S.O., a job with his family's business, and a position with University Christian Outreach in Pittsburgh, Pennsylvania as a U.C.O. Coordinator. "I jumped at the opportunity to work with university students on a different campus, I thought it would be a fresh opportunity to meet people and help them to develop their Christian faith. I considered it a privilege to take a spiritual concern when working with college students, and to work in cooperation with God in their lives."

University Christian Outreach (U.C.O.) in Pittsburgh serves students from the Oakland area, which encompasses four major universities and a community college. Students from the University of Pittsburgh, Carnegie Mellon University, and Duquesne University are members. U.C.O. is a Christian group that concentrates on teaching college students about the Bible, Jesus' teachings, and Christian discipleship (faith formation in an adult setting). It provides opportunity for friendship, small groups, and fellowship in recreational activities. Ross's role was to coordinate meetings, activities, retreats and outings, and to facilitate communication between U.C.O. staff and the local Christian group which provides funding for the U.C.O. Pittsburgh chapter. He was also responsible for assigning weekly tasks and responsibilities for other U.C.O. staff.

"Most of all, my years working for U.C.O. helped me to process through how I saw other people. It helped me to learn to love and accept people exactly where they are "right now" and to see that God's love for each person is not predicated on what they do - but on that they are. They exist because God created them from love and allowed them to be. So, it was my goal to find something to love about each person in U.C.O. - and beyond. Later, my work with foreign university students would further expand my ability to love and understand people with disparate backgrounds, experiences and languages. U.C.O. was work that taught me how to love."

Although Ross's transition from college to work life was circuitous, it was uncomplicated. And although Ross really enjoyed working for U.C.O., he felt led in a different direction eventually, and started taking computer courses at the Community College of Allegheny County and eventually applied to the University to Pittsburgh. Having completed his master's degree in Information Science at the University of Pittsburgh in December of 2015, Ross is looking for a full-time professional position and will transition out of university mission work. His pastoral worker (supervisor) and personal prayer have helped him to discern that seeking work in academia is not realistic (financially) because of how long it would take him to reach a sustainable salary which would pay his rent, student loans and other expenses. So far, his job search in Pittsburgh has not yielded a job offer that would meet his financial needs, so he will continue looking until he finds a realistic work arrangement. "If I need to leave Pittsburgh to find a good job, I will have to adjust my expectations; most of my friends are here, and I would like to stay if I am able." Ross may have to work an unpaid internship to get work experience, while also working a fulltime entry position, but he is prepared to do that if necessary. "If I had hopped on getting an internship a year earlier, I may have had more focus and clarity on what type of I.T. (Information Technology) jobs that I was interested in."

What type of advice would Ross give to a loved one who is discerning what type of field to go into? "Try to understand who you are in the broader story of Creation; have your identity rooted in God. What is your own personal true calling? Even if it is out of your comfort zone, faith of some kind is always involved in following your call. Lastly: what are the practical or strategic pros and cons of any of your potential paths? Map it out, write it down, and then ask a friend or family member who knows you well. At the end though: it really is your own decision that you are going to live with."

Regarding his own immediate future, Ross says this: "I want to have a professional I.T. job and get a couple of years of experience to establish my work portfolio, be financially secure, and be married. Anything further than that is too far away to see."

Chapter 4:
Second Careers: Unique Challenges

It is becoming more common that people decide to completely change course in their careers, and companies are also now more likely to pressure existing employees to advance to college education, their college graduates to master degrees, and to expect older employees to be more portable and computer-savvy. These shifting expectations can create a "moving target" approach when an individual employee is considering "Should I stay, or should I go?"

There are complex and varied reasons as to why people change career paths midstream: increased financial responsibilities, a change in personal focus and values, unexpected job loss, discontent, job instability, even geographic relocation. These precipitating factors may be perceived as the perfect opportunity to make a change, to get a fresh start and perspective. There are some employees, however, who experience a vast paradigm shift that seems to come from inside of themselves, and which precipitates a major vocational change:

Father Ken Marlovits: Heeding a Higher Call

I meet with Father Ken Marlovits in his parish office, a small, sun-filled space on the campus of a large Roman Catholic parish within minutes of downtown Pittsburgh. Father Ken has a calm and easy way about him, affable and curious. He looks younger than his 44 years, has a firm grip and an open posture. He asks a few questions about the book, gives me some insight into his role at the parish, and we begin.

Having had many rewarding years of service to the public education system, one would think that Ken Marlovits would have continued the more natural course of his original vocation as teacher (and then school administrator), but Father Ken heeded a supernatural call, his true vocational call.

Ken Marlovits attended Penn State after high school, and graduated in 1992. "I became a social studies teacher at Blackhawk High School the following year, and then enjoyed ten years as a teacher there before earning my master's degree in Education, which gained me a promotion to Assistant Principal of the school." That year became a searching year for him, in which he felt called in another direction (an inner tugging that said to him "there is something more for you"). One of the instigators of this discovery was spending time in church experiencing Eucharistic Adoration for an hour every week (for one of his activities as the head of his local Knights of Columbus chapter). Eucharistic Adoration is the practice of praying in a church or chapel while the Communion Host is set on the altar. It is a method of contemplative prayer unique to Roman Catholic believers. Ken's Knights of Columbus chapter was assigned to pray specifically for the provision of young men and women as future nuns and priests. "I never imagined that I would be one of the people who received a vocational call because of Eucharistic Adoration, but I did know that I was searching for something more." He was in the Denial Stage of Fisher's Process, sensing that there was a big change ahead, but denying what that might mean for his life.

By this time, Ken was already almost 36 years old, and thought that he had his whole career trajectory mapped out. He didn't expect that the extra weekly hour of prayer, and consultation with a Spiritual Director, would help point him to his true call, that of an ordained priest. "I very much enjoyed my position at Blackhawk, and part of that job was to help students and parents who were searching for improvement for their own lives." That set an early spark with him, that true authentic life needs to include spiritual development and fulfillment, not just temporal fulfillment. Ken truly experienced a choice between two good paths, and realized that the joy that he experienced from helping the parents and their children came from a spiritual place: "Sometimes your heart desires more than a job."

"During the year in which I discerned whether to leave my position at Blackhawk, one of the things that I kept in mind was that I felt an obligation to my local community." He knew that because he was a hometown school administrator, some people would be incredulous or disappointed in his decision to leave his position as Assistant Principal. Nevertheless, "I sensed that I was following a call, a vocation to set aside other people's expectations and plans for my life, and that I desired first to be where God could use me as an instrument for Him." At this point, Ken experienced the Moving Forward stage of Fisher's Process, making specific plans to leave behind his former career.

At the age of 37, Father Ken entered seminary to receive training and direction as a priest-in-training. He had taken an Intro to Catholicism course at the seminary during his year of searching that had put him in touch with a Vocational Director, who helped to guide him through the application process. "I eventually also had a very good Spiritual Director/counselor at the theological college, who was trained to help us seminarians wrestle with life issues," including those that arise from family of origin. This is a very important aspect of seminary life, that these issues be worked out before priests are ordained.

Father Ken acknowledged that once a man enters the seminary, there is a tremendous amount of pressure to progress along until ordination. But equally as clear, that there are many people praying for seminarians, and that each seminarian is human and not perfect. In that part of his vocational training, Father Ken experienced the Gradual Acceptance Stage: "Many priests, including me, have experienced being honed on, especially when we are wearing our collars. We become targets, either for prayer requests, attention, or for negative and angry comments." In a sense, each priest "disappears" behind the collar, and they become symbolic instead of being seen as a "regular" human being; for many people, even for non-Catholics, a collar is seen as the universal symbol of holiness or of being set apart for God's work. "For me, I had already experienced that as an Assistant Principal, disappearing behind a job title. So I didn't feel as keenly the loss of a singular identity as other priests might." In fact, on the day of his ordination, he felt the identity shift: "I am now a priest."

However, it wasn't until four years into seminary that Father Ken saw himself as a teacher of the faith instead of a teacher of curriculum! That part of himself had become second-nature to him. "I also wrestled with the idea that faith formation is not concrete, but amorphous, which requires my role to be more passive; I have had to become a better listener, and to learn to put my teacher role on the shelf." He came to see himself as an observer of others' faith paths, which happened in the last year of his seminary training. Father Ken had become a "guide to faith" instead of a teacher of information. He was in the Moving Forward Stage.

Although Father Ken is confident that he chose the right vocation, he misses his fellow teachers, their shared struggles and goals, and the students. He doesn't miss that teaching has become about testing, not the shared goal of acquiring knowledge. Also, Father Ken has been able to use his teaching and administrative gifts in his position as Parochial Vicar, because his current parish also operates a school. "My vocation marries the two parts of myself, teacher and spiritual guide. And I am on this journey as well, learning more about God, his people and our faith, every day. I should never stop learning, never become stagnant."

All along this transformational path, his faith in God, his Spiritual Director, and the supportive prayers of his loved ones have borne him up. "I have learned that when I let the Holy Spirit guide me, that other people see that, and positively respond to it."

Father Ken's biggest identity shift came from realizing that as he left his job and moved on with his seminary training, his previous friends and co-workers had changed, moved, and moved along in their lives. "I rarely reconnect with my old teaching team and when I do, there are new faces, new babies, new jobs and new dreams. It's pretty hard for me to keep up with all of it, and maybe - I'm not meant to." As Father Ken, now age 44, has moved onward and upward, so have the people who comprised his old life.

These little griefs are something that he has shared with, and processed through, a small group of priests who share the same griefs, trials, joys and transformations. They are a group of men with whom he feels totally comfortable sharing every aspect of priestly life, and the small group is a peer-oriented and reciprocal support in which he feels completely safe and authentic. From new seminarian to deacon to ordained priest, what they have together is more than friendship, it is a shared life's path.

Father Ken's advice is this: "Trust that no matter what, you ARE resilient enough to bounce back from taking a risk in changing your career or vocation. And, do not let the fear of 'what if' control your decisions."

Lisa Toboz: Pack it Up, Pack it In

Lisa Toboz and I meet in her storefront shotgun-style apartment in a Pittsburgh city neighborhood that is currently experiencing the sweeping impact of gentrification. Lisa's Eastern European ethnic background has gifted her with long, thick hair and exotic eyes; her curvy vintage dresses and one-of-a-kind shoe styles show her neo-feminism flair.

Lisa's building has been well-maintained, but the crumbling, abandoned building next door has presented some challenges to its neighbors, including the need periodically trap mice that Lisa's cat Lulu seems to be completely baffled by. "Jeff and I have been married since 2008 and love living in a city environment (although the parking issues can be annoying)." The decor is eclectic, charming, and neatly kept. Their home is fronted by display windows in which she and her husband periodically display other artists' work, including miniature dioramas, sculptures, drawing and photography. Lisa and Jeff have been enthusiastically involved in the Pittsburgh art community for many years, Lisa as a writer and photographer, Jeff in a band and a designer of handmade guitars. Lisa and Jeff have extensive circles of friends, and fulfilling careers.

But for Lisa, her most impactful vocational transition came in 2004, in the form of an extreme whole-life overhaul. For the previous seven years, she had worked at a local lifestyle newspaper as a bookkeeper; her bachelor's degree in English went unused in that position, and she was weary of office dynamics and politics. She had entered the Disillusionment stage of Fisher's Process: she had reached an awareness that her personal goals, values, and beliefs were no longer compatible with that of her work environment.

"I had researched different volunteer positions, and was drawn to a teaching opportunity in Croatia, at the Center for Peace. A whole set of things fell into place: a friend of mine coming back from Tokyo agreed to take over my apartment, I had a 401k to use for the plane ticket and living expenses, and I had hit a point where I just needed to get away from my life to get some peace, to travel, and be somewhere new." There were other, more personal reasons, too: Lisa's mother's struggles with mental illness felt like they were closing in on Lisa, sometimes making her feel claustrophobic and pressured to be in the parental role.

The other consideration? Lisa was getting ready to turn 30, and many of her friends were getting married and having children, but those life choices were not even on Lisa's radar.

Lisa had begun the Happiness Stage: "Everything pointed to Croatia."

Lisa applied and was accepted to the volunteer program. "I packed my belongings away, put in my work resignation, and prepared myself mentally for the big adventure ahead." In the meantime, her plan faced skepticism from her family. Lisa grew up in a blue-collar neighborhood in a working-class family: "they didn't understand why I aspired to be more, to do more, than the generation before me." Somehow her educational and career aspirations were interpreted to mean that Lisa thought she was better than the rest of her family. Some family members felt that her plan was not practical, and she perceived that they thought she was not grown up enough to make such radical decisions. There was also an almost xenophobic tinge to some responses: "Why Croatia? Why go halfway across the world to help people? Isn't it dangerous there?"

Lisa had been pen pals with her Slovenian friend Tamara since she was 13 years old, and wasn't afraid to go to Eastern Europe. She knew a bit about the Dayton Accord, which was a peace agreement that afforded an end of war actions between Croatia, Yugoslavia, and Bosnia; and that Accord had opened the door for war crimes to be tried through the courts of the United Nations. "I was intrigued by the significant depth of history and culture in Croatia, and was excited to have the opportunity to enter into everyday life" through volunteer service.

"What I didn't know about (and so couldn't plan for) was the closed-off society that Croatia had become in the years between 1995 and 2004. Croatia's infrastructure had experienced extensive damage due to war, and its transportation, communication and commerce systems were drastically affected." And so, as she arrived in Osijek, Croatia after a short sightseeing jaunt in Hungary and Zagreb, Croatia, she wasn't prepared for the isolation and loneliness that awaited her. She had stepped into the Denial Stage: "This is bigger than I thought!" and "Did I really do this??"

In those years before widespread Internet use, the bulk of Lisa's information about the town and her volunteer program had come from the program itself. Lisa didn't know that Osijek was an isolated town surrounded by farmland, with unreliable bus service and minimal post-war recovery of the commercial infrastructure. She was also rebounding from an uncomfortable sightseeing trip with an old paramour from Ireland; "he wanted to visit Croatia and to see me, and so I agreed to go on the sightseeing trip with him before starting my volunteer job. It was not the right move. I was trying to shed the skin of my old life; and he was troubled, insecure and flighty."

Regardless of Lisa's shaky start, Croatia soon became the best choice she had made in a long time. She made several new friends soon after moving to Osijek, friends that became life support to her while in a foreign land. She was again in the stage of Happiness in Fisher's Process.

After an adjustment period to the expectations of her new position, she came to enjoy her teaching experiences and her students. But what was most impactful was the wholescale effect that her time in Croatia had on her life: "that trip, that experience, was the turning point for many other events in my life. It set off a purposeful shift in my personal and artistic approaches, and it kindled my interest in journaling my experiences through photography (rather than through writing)." Lisa had kept a journal since she was a preteen, and had scores of notebooks and hardbound journals as testimony to her past. But Croatia sparked an interest in, and love for, the craft of photography. Photography soon replaced journaling as her primary way of keeping memories and experiences alive.

Croatia also showed her the depth of what international travel had to offer, the human link to people whom she had never met before and didn't have natural connections to, but whom affected her life regardless. There was Ari, a friend of hers who found a small Jewish community in Osijek that he connected with; "Andrija and Irana, a couple who lived in nearby Tenja who became a makeshift family for me during my stay"; a psychologist who worked with local war victims, a bizarre character who had no social skills but tried to convince Ari to stay in Osijek permanently; and an elderly man who had escaped the Holocaust by leaving Croatia via the Adriatic Sea to Trieste, Italy. All these supportive individuals helped to weave the fabric of her Croatian experience, and that adventurous year helped propel her into a new job back in the United States and into the Moving Forward stage of Fisher's Process.

Hindsight being 20/20, Lisa (age 42), does have some regrets about her trip Croatia. She felt that she didn't research access to surrounding towns, and her ability to travel outside of Osijek was limited by the crippled infrastructure of transportation resulting from the war. She also should have done better financial planning (saving, etc.) while preparing for the trip. Lisa wishes she was braver about traveling while she was there, "just to get on a train on my day off, and see where it took me." While in Croatia, she was sometimes in the Fear or Anger stages of Fisher's Process, many times because of things that happened that were out of her control, or were not anticipated. Lisa regrets not having more purposeful adventures and experiences, and not putting more of a photographic emphasis on the trip. But you can't go back, only forward; and Lisa has some advice for those considering similar experiences.

"Have a solid financial plan. Have a focus to what you are doing. If you are young enough, you can take some risks in your life. You never want to get to be old and say 'I wish I had done ___.' If you ask me, 'should I?' I will always say 'Yes'."

Lisa is incredibly grateful to all those people who supported her plan, who believed in her and her intention for the trip to Croatia. "I had a very supportive supervisor at the newspaper, who understood why I had to leave my job, and helped me out financially when I returned stateside." Lisa's network of friends and fellow employees were also very encouraging and supportive, and she received many emails while in Croatia from them and some of their parents, which felt like a hug from home. She also had friends who sent packages of clothing and supplies for the students in her class. The support of these people helped her to have the confidence to see her dream come to fruition, and Croatia "helped expose my independence, my strength and my fortitude. It developed me into an artist, instead of simply - a worker. My job now, it pays the bills, but my **identity** is in photography."

Even if you are excited about a new career path and its possibilities, it can feel at first as if you are pretending, going through the motions for the sake of the company, a kind of "fake it till you make it" mentality, which Marisol N. experienced first-hand:

Marisol N.*: Burning out on Human Services work

Marisol N.* is an intelligent and attractive woman who spontaneously smiles, and engages me in fast-paced conversation. We meet in her modest apartment in a suburb of Pittsburgh on the second floor of a brick home, neat and within walking distance of the borough's downtown area. The area is full of local boutique businesses, like reasonably-priced antiques, old-style barber shops, small bakeries and discreet tattoo parlors. It is a typical middle-class Pittsburgh suburb, with the surrounding main road full of chain restaurants and gas stations, and signs for ramps to the connecting highways. In such towns, you can hear three separate sounds that bounce off the surrounding hills: trains, planes, and highway traffic. The sounds become background noise after a few months of living in these crossroad boroughs. Marisol grew up in this town, and is comfortable here.

"I always knew that I wanted to work in education or social work!", Marisol offers. She graduated from Penn State University, taught in a high school for a year, and then went on to work for Goodwill Industries as a Student Support Services/Case Worker for four and a half years. "I then left Goodwill to pursue a position as a career advisor at a local job training program that is funded and run by the U.S. Department of Labor." She held that job for more than four years, but after a total of nine years working in human service agencies, found herself in the Disillusionment stage of Fisher's Process.

Marisol, now age 38, had begun her time at the job training program on a very positive note. She was optimistic that she would be able to help her clients to transition from lives of poverty and misdirection, to lives of purpose and vocation. "Instead, I found that I was expected to treat my clients as if they were 'product' instead of people; and I often had to sell this uncompleted product to job sites that really needed mature, well-trained workers ready to hit the ground running."

Marisol's experience of co-workers was somewhat negative, as well. She discovered that her Christian identity was often expected to be subsumed in favor of a bland office environment, and non-Christian co-workers sometimes chastised or teased her for her Christian beliefs. Marisol understood that she couldn't evangelize her clients, but was certain that personal religious identity and expression shouldn't have been a taboo subject, regardless of who her employer was. She also gradually became frustrated, demoralized and bewildered at the lack of progress in her clients, and after four and a half years as a career advisor, was convinced that it was time to move on, preferably to a work environment outside of social work. Studies have proven that human services workers experience burnout at a much higher rate than other employees, and that recognizing and addressing early symptoms of burnout can reduce sick leave and disability claims (Borritz, 2010).

At the encouragement of friends, family, and her Christian community's small group members, Marisol decided to pursue a position with a manufacturing company's corporate office. She had heard about an executive assistant position becoming available, and decided to jump at the chance to leave her social work career behind. She sent her resume to the company in December of 2013, and then forgot about it.

In mid-March of 2014, Marisol received a call from one of the company's vice presidents, who wanted to do a phone interview with her. The company was particularly interested in Marisol's bilingual skills, and had clients in Mexico and other areas that might benefit from her background in that area. She then proceeded to an in-person interview with the vice president, and everything progressed from there; she was offered the position shortly thereafter.

"Through all of these decisions and changes, I prayed to God constantly," Marisol says. She prayed that she was making the right choice, to leave her previous position and social work career; that she could perform well in a new, unfamiliar environment and position; and that the environment would be more positive, challenging and focused than her time at the job training program. Marisol was confident that a change was exactly what she needed, and was in the Happiness Stage of Fisher's Process.

Marisol also knew that this career would look far different than her human services career, and hoped that she was up to the task. A company that is focused on quality products and profits operates far differently than those agencies whose "products" are people. And the need for precision work and a good rapport with outside clients was made clear to her, even very early on. Until she got comfortable in this new environment, Marisol operated in the stage of Anxiety from Fisher's Process, as she did not have enough information to anticipate what all of the expectations or feedback would be.

"My initial support for this transition came from a friend at the manufacturing company who encouraged me to apply, told me that I could definitely do the job, and then encouraged me in the new job as I adjusted to the new atmosphere and responsibilities." Additionally, her small group provided encouragement as she experienced the initial awkwardness at shifting from a non-profit environment to a for-profit company. Marisol's father helped her with technical support while updating her resume, and her parents and sister served as moral support. Her small group leader gave her feedback on how to ask for an appropriate salary and other pertinent, practical questions before she interviewed face to face.

Marisol's advice to anyone in similar circumstances? "Don't put all your identity in your work. Follow your dreams and don't give up on them; find out what the concrete steps are that you have to take in order to get there, and then take it one step at a time. Also, give yourself time to properly sift out the different voices in your head: what is ego? what is lack of confidence? how might God be speaking to you about this decision?"

"I don't miss my old job at all, and I know that I made the right decision to leave human services behind." Marisol is in the Gradual Acceptance stage of Fisher's Process. She is still waiting to see what the rest of her life and vocational path will turn out to be, and is enjoying the challenges and her new position as she figures that out.

Kate Grella: Being Your Own Boss Takes Some Getting Used To

Kate Grella and I meet in her home, a sunny split-level atop large hills in the suburbs of Pittsburgh, close to the Allegheny/Washington county line. Her neighborhood was part farmland, part housing developments until just a few years ago. Now the adjoining horse farm has been fenced in on all sides by new development. You are now just as likely to see minivans on that road as you are to see turkey and deer. Kate is a six-foot, blonde and blue-eyed vivacious woman who speaks animatedly. Her interview ends at a little over two hours, as we both have similar conversation styles and love to talk. Kate has very strong opinions, and an even stronger desire to be a loving Christian, great wife and mother.

For Kate Grella (age 35), working as a Director of Religious Education (D.R.E.) for a parish in the Diocese of Pittsburgh used to fit squarely into her comfort zone, her training, her education and her personal and professional gifts. "Being responsible for the development, coordination and teaching of religious education for Catholic church members 'from cradle to grave' is a rewarding (and sometimes exhausting) vocation. But I absolutely craved the opportunity to be at home with our two small children, and paying for childcare for multiple children out of my modest salary just didn't make sense." She was in the Disillusionment Phase of Fisher's Process ("I need to leave, this isn't for me.")

The transition to staying home with her children was meant to be gradual; Kate resigned her fulltime position, and continued to work part time (approximately five to ten hours per week) for a year as the Director of Sacramental Preparation. "However, my successor couldn't give me the day during the week that I wanted to work; I feel that she wanted to supervise my work, even though I had been a D.R.E. for over ten years. It was very difficult to compromise with someone who didn't want to meet me halfway, so instead, I worked at night and on weekends, which affected my family time and my time with my husband." Kate found herself in the Anger Stage soon after she had resigned her fulltime position.

Kate continued to feel the tug-and-pull of her previous position, as she watched her successor dismantle or change many of the longstanding parish programs and family supports that Kate had worked for years to develop. Kate was never asked to train her successor, nor to explain to her the value of each of the programs, and so felt that it was the pastor's duty to supervise the new DRE and to give her direction about how things would (or should) happen. She felt that she had to watch her previous mission field get deconstructed before her very eyes, and it was painful.

Regarding her home life position, Kate was in the Depression Phase of Fisher's Process: she was experiencing growing pains in her new position as a stay at home mom and had discomfort some days, which was confusing to her husband, as she had chosen to be at home, and so why was it hard to adjust? "I didn't know how to structure my days anymore! Sometimes I felt lost in the chaos of the day, and the mood and the needs of the kids sometimes sets not only the priorities of the day, but the schedule of the day. I felt a little lost at first, to be honest." Additionally, Kate was missing the camaraderie of the workplace. Her assistant at work had been her constant support and companion, and they had shared a very easy friendship together. The loss of that daily rapport was difficult. Life in parish support has a specific language, and Kate had lost that language from her daily life. Also, some friendships were harder to maintain because she had left their shared "language" behind.

Kate has other friends who have been in similar situations, so talking to those women helped her to normalize her experience. Their friendship - and commiseration - allowed Kate to see that what she was going through was manageable and temporary. "By the time I again reduced my hours, this time to ten hours per month and limiting my involvement to the Catholic adult initiation program, I had gotten into a groove. My youngest was only three months old when I quit my fulltime job, and so I felt that I didn't miss any milestones with her, but caring for an infant and two small children, all under the age of five - your days just go so quickly! But about a year into working part time, I had become more organized and structured in my weekday schedule, and things became more predictable and manageable." She does concede that she misses the work lunches and other outings without her kids in tow, and the adult interaction and verbal encouragement from her peers, and she has to make extra effort to see her former assistant; they are now only able to get together a few times a year.

Emotionally, Kate saw a change when she adjusted to resigning her position. She became less anxious and worrisome, concentrated her emotional and mental energy on her family life, and felt more calm and centered. Kate also saw that once she had asserted her position at work, and gained more mastery in her work decisions and schedule, that she became less of a people-pleaser and more her own person. There was no time or space to do that whenever she had been working 50+ hours per week!

Spiritually, Kate saw an improvement in feeling more centered and she had more time to pray during the day. She also had more time to foster her friendships with other stay at home mothers, and enjoys the opportunity to share playdates with their children, or lunches together.

Kate doesn't miss the harried pace of the working mom's morning which involved getting the girls and their gear packed and ready to go to the sitter's house, having to drive to work in bad winter weather, and missing important milestones in her children's lives. She also doesn't feel the weight of responsibility of a whole parish's faith formation: "Some of the parents that I dealt with in the catechism program felt that the classes were simply an interruption in their children's sports schedule! WOW."

Kate misses her full income sometimes, especially when considering the financial implications of more children or a bigger house. Also, she used to be able to watch the impressive faith progression of whole families; progress in her own children, because she sees them every day, seems less obvious. But Kate knows that the unique opportunity to stay at home and raise her own children, is not to be taken for granted. Now she is in the Gradual Acceptance stage of Fisher's Process: she is making sense of her working environment, and of her place within the vocational change.

Kate has advice for parents who are considering setting aside their careers to stay at home with their children: "You have to realize that it's okay to be unhappy at first, and you should expect it to not be perfect. Just make a plan to structure your days, so that it's not like your pace drops off of a cliff! Do work in yourself ahead of time regarding the changes in your identity, and plan for time for yourself, including maybe even a hobby (I started a wine club with my friends). Give it time, and understand that it is what is best for your kids."

Kate's future vocational plans include waiting until all of her children are off to college, and then going back to work for the local diocese: "I see it as a living organism, not an organization, and would really look forward to being a part of the growth of the church again."

Katie Hilbert: My Marriage Didn't Fit, and Neither Did My Job

It was 2014, and for the first time, Katie Hilbert was living alone. Katie had progressed from her family home to college to marriage and all along the way, shared space. Katie was now faced with divorce, silence and even more, the mental space to work it all out: "What did I want? Where was my career going? Was I okay being alone and sometimes, lonely? After my marriage of ten years had ended, what else did I need to take another look at?"

After Katie's dysfunctional marriage ended, her friend gave her a reference to a therapist. This therapist helped Katie to evaluate where to go next with her life, partly through self-evaluation, but also, through spending time in meditation (for physical calmness) and oral journaling (by using voice-to-text options on her cell phone). These tools, along with therapy appointments, helped Katie to evaluate what she wanted to do next: "What impact do I want to make in my career? The answer was: a combination of ecology, food and food systems policy."

"My current job is as a Farmers Market Manager/Coordinator with a CSA (Community Supported Agriculture) organization. A majority of my job is farmer's market coordination of our products and phone contact with our customers. I don't necessarily feel that I am having as much impact in people's lives, compared to being in the fields of Eco-Psychology or Horticulture Therapy, which is where I think I'm headed with my career. Both fields guide people to a strong connection with the land, by educating them about where their food comes from, and how the earth can help to heal and ground them psychologically and in other ways." Regarding her current career, Katie has reached the Disillusionment stage of Fisher's Process: "I'm off! This isn't for me."

Katie has given the CSA ample notice, so that they know to replace her, or to find someone whom she can train into her position. She has talked to her supervisor, and has discovered that she may be able to collect unemployment benefits while she networks for new jobs and builds ideas around where to go next. Katie is open to moving out of Pennsylvania, or even out of the United States, "I'd love to live in another country for a while, maybe South Africa. The States seem parochial, narrow-minded, closed to radical ideas. There's no global feel in the States, it sort of has an us-against-them feel, at least politically."

Katie credits the therapeutic process for her awakening to career possibilities. "Before I was in therapy, I couldn't see that my job didn't fit my life anymore. Initially, having a job that physically engaged me helped me to feel empowered, especially during the divorce. It just doesn't suit me anymore. I want to work in a field where I am helping people to meet more than just their physical needs, but also their psychological and spiritual needs." Katie feels that her therapist, her friends, and her professional cohorts (who help link her to the Pittsburgh food scene), have all been supportive. Two of the coping skills that have worked very well for her are dating a younger man (which has been a distraction from her job ambivalence), and being involved with a local gospel choir. Her choir has public performances between 12 and 15 times per year, and she finds that she feels more connected to the Pittsburgh community as she gets to know the choir members. "And when we sing, our heart rates coincide! There's an almost primal connectedness, we all feel lifted up and ALIVE. This has helped to validate for me that people ARE connected, that none of us are on the journey of life alone."

There are many things that Katie will miss about working with the CSA team. "Being welcomed into different Pittsburgh communities, with different cultures and the experiences there, I will miss that. I'll miss our connection to growers, that our cooperation makes it possible for small farms to stay in business and to get their produce to people who are looking to improve their physical health. I'll miss the easy days at the Farmers Market stands. I also enjoy being responsible for having an integral link in the food chain."

Katie advises "Know yourself and what you need to be happy: what are your values? Question everything. Don't sleepwalk through your marriage, your career, or any part of your life. Don't assume that other people will fulfill your needs. Do take natural steps towards your destiny by asking advice from people you trust, and whom have good intentions towards you. If you need more formal help, don't be afraid to seek the advice of a counselor. I know it makes people feel vulnerable, but put yourself 'out there'. Don't discredit yourself, or what you are capable of. Be honest with yourself! And lastly: Dream Big! Your passion + your goal = Fulfillment!"

Patty Wihlborg: Motherhood In My 40's Was A Challenge

Patty Wihlborg and I meet in a bright and bustling Panera Bread, the buzz of conversation all around us. Patty's quick smile and natural beauty really shine, as we jump from greeting to book description to interview questions. Her consideration of each question shows that she is interested in discussing all angles of her vocational experience, so that I can see and sketch out her full story.

"I am not your typical stay-at-home mom," says Patty Wihlborg. As a new college graduate from Indiana University of Pennsylvania (IUP) in 1981, she had entered the workforce with her bachelors in Management of Information Systems. She worked a traditional position until a year after she married her husband, Will, in 1998 (17 years later). She then worked from home full-time from 1999 until 2001, and by then Patty and Will had two little children.

"When I became pregnant with our second child in 2000, I started wondering whether my salary was worth the trouble of trying to work a full-time job from home - while also trying to raise two small children." Patty went on maternity leave in 2001, and she nervously called the corporate office in Boston; the company had just been sold, and the new owners were interested in simplifying operations. They asked Patty to transition out of her job by helping them through the corporate transition, as Patty's input was integral to their data transfer and process/software transition. They offered her a considerable salary increase for her troubles, and she accepted the offer. Shortly thereafter, she "retired."

When Patty and Will's older child began preschool, Patty went through a typical "honeymoon" phase with being a stay-at-home mom; she liked being in charge of her own domestic destiny, having free time with the kids, and taking full control of her household. But then doubt set in, and Patty often found herself thinking, "WHY am I doing this again??" She realized that the lack of structure in her day often left her feeling unmoored, and so took very specific action to change that, including joining a gym, a group called M.O.P.S. (Mothers of Preschoolers), and a parish-based bible study. Having more structure to her days (and more contact with other adults) helped Patty to feel more grounded, more sociable, and less "lost" in her new stay at home role.

"M.O.P.S. was especially helpful to me because the group's moms watched the children in groups on a rotating basis, and the other moms were freed up to socialize, do a craft or other team building activity, talk about parenting or other issues, and build friendships with each other." M.O.P.S. also presented an opportunity for Patty and the other women to pray for each other, make new friends, and find connection with other Christian moms. "As important as the other benefits, M.O.P.S. helped me to see my new role as a fulltime mother to be valuable, worthy, and a higher calling; that prioritizing the development of my children over career aspirations would benefit our whole family." Some of these proven benefits to children include: consistent bonding between child and mother (especially in the first five years, it is critically important to the physical and social development of children) (Tronick, 1975), more positive neural development in babies' brains in the first two years, lower rates of baby and toddler anxiety and stress (Mooney, 2013), lower rates of depression in adolescence, and lower rates of antisocial behavior in adolescence (Mooney, 2013).

Although Patty sacrificed some parts of her adult identity in order to raise her children fulltime, she fully appreciated that her choice to entirely embrace her motherly role (instead of having her children in childcare) benefited her children. But she came to see that she also benefited from her role. Patty had the time, energy, and connections to make new friends and create new support systems. She was free to eventually volunteer at her children's schools, and as a school board member. "I didn't have to second-guess my children's caretaking arrangements, take off of work for sick children, or wonder whether the constant tug-and-pull between a fulltime job and parenting was ever worth it." She also didn't miss the very long work days that came from (originally) being a single person with no children, because the pressure to work longer hours in that state of life was obvious to her.

Some of the less positive aspects of transitioning to full-time parenting were that she was more likely to procrastinate once she was her own boss; that "I missed the intellectual stimulation from interacting with work cohorts, because most of my adult interaction began to be from casual interactions with other school parents, there was a built-in system of connection there"; the mental stimulation of structured and high-pressure work assignments, and the validation from being good at her job; and the financial differences of having one family salary vs. two.

Patty's next anticipated vocational transition is part-time work to save money for her daughters' college tuition. "I have a lot of free time now, my daughters don't need as much personal attention, and college is has become very expensive and I would like to help them to avoid large student loans." This desire reflects a newer trend in parental assistance with children's college tuition: paying as they go, instead of co-signing more student loans (Douglas-Gabriel, 2015).

Patty's advice to other stay at home parents is this: "I highly recommend finding part-time work or volunteer work, as this naturally creates a situation where your younger kids can experience preschool or informal group interactions with other children before they go to kindergarten. It also creates a better mental and emotional balance for yourself. You look forward to seeing your kids again if you aren't with them 24/7."

Another consideration, ahead of time? "If you are married, make sure you work on your marriage, before and after kids. Prioritize communication with each other, especially on budgeting and parenting topics. A solid marriage is more likely to predict a successful transition for someone who wants to be a stay at home parent."

Chrissy Thompson: Practicality, Strength and Independence*

For Chrissy Thompson, it's a tossup as to whether transitioning from military to civilian life, or married to single life, was the most 'memorable'. One transition she was very prepared for: leaving military life behind. The other, not so much: she had only been married for nine years, and her son was two years old when she divorced, and that process was rougher than she anticipated.

In 1971, Chrissy was a fresh-faced sophomore at a university in Pittsburgh, studying nursing. "My sorority sister's father was at the Pentagon during the Vietnam War, and communicated through her that the federal government desperately needed medical personnel overseas. We decided to apply for the available tuition scholarships, and were both accepted." The friends graduated from university in 1973, enjoyed the summer, and in September both headed to San Antonio, Texas for six weeks of U.S. Army Basic Training. After Basic Training, Chrissy requested to be sent to Vietnam, but instead was sent to Monterey, California to Fort Ord.

"That's where I met my husband. He was a respiratory therapist at Fort Ord. After we got married, he was given orders in 1975 to proceed to Honolulu, Hawaii to Tripler Army Medical and the Schofield Barracks Emergency Room." He was to be assigned for three years, so Chrissy decided to re-up (extend her length of military service). By early 1977, Chrissy's husband had completed his military time, so he began work as a civilian respiratory therapist on base, and eventually transitioned to a civilian hospital.

"At the same time, we were looking forward to my contract release in April of 1978. We decided that we would move to Pittsburgh (near my family) after my time was up, and in preparation for that, completely banked one of our salaries so that we could buy a home as soon as we returned to Pennsylvania. I'm a planner by nature, I like the logistics that go into a long-term plan, and I like being financially prepared. I'm very practical, and sometimes brutally honest; that combination can create problems in friendships with other women, and I also don't get attached very easily. That's probably due to my military experience, but also due to my nursing career. You learn to be logical and detached to do your job efficiently and in a practical way."

Chrissy and her husband sold their home in Hawaii in the spring of 1978, and purchased a home in the suburbs of Pittsburgh, Pennsylvania. Chrissy soon procured a position at a weight loss clinic and her husband worked as a respiratory therapist. By 1980 they had added a son to their family, and shortly thereafter, marital tensions became more intense. "The main reason we got divorced in '82 was that away from military life, the difference in our family values became more obvious. We also worked opposite shifts and didn't see each other enough. I think that's common with married people who are in healthcare positions; they are fast-paced jobs, can be high-stress. We had different faith values, too. The whole time we lived in Hawaii, I attended a Catholic church that had a family feel to it. The priest was great! But my husband didn't attend. That wasn't good for us."

Chrissy divorced in 1982 and lived in her home with her young son. She purposefully looked for a job that would give her a stable 9-to-5 shift so that her schedule would be predictable. "I stayed in jobs that I didn't love, and as long as they were day jobs and had decent salaries, that's all that mattered to me." She ended up in the Home Health Care field, which provided a good salary and allowed her to work day shifts, no weekends necessary. "I went into some pretty rotten house conditions. I had to serve six to seven clients per shift, no matter how far apart they lived. I did get compensated for mileage, but didn't feel that I was giving my clients what they deserved, the kind of attention that I would want if I needed home health care."

Chrissy persisted in her field until 1991, when a hemangioma was found on her liver. The mass was very vascular, and Chrissy was given a 50/50 chance of making it out of surgery. Chrissy survived, and upon returning to work, was transferred to another department. Chrissy decided to leave that company and apply for an office job somewhere else.

Upon reflection, Chrissy said "Nursing jobs are pretty much the same, whether in or out of the military. My identity was as a nurse first, not as military personnel. I mean, I enjoyed the military benefits, but there wasn't much difference in my actual job functions when I became a civilian again." She also noted that there are the same kind of job 'politics' in a regular job, as there is in the military. "And just in time to retire, you finally master your career," she laughs.

To anyone who may transition from military to civilian life, Chrissy advises, "It's all about the planning and logistics! You need to consider financial, housing, job options. For me, I believe in myself and that I am capable of doing what needs to be done. I make a plan and I execute it. You also need to tap into available supports. I have lifelong friends, and when I got back to Pittsburgh from Hawaii, my parents were especially supportive."

Having recently retired, Chrissy continues to keep herself busy: "I do whatever I want, when I want! And I volunteer frequently. I'm not the type to sit at home and wait to die."

Angela Gross: Developing a Career from a Hobby

Angela Gross and I meet at a small, pristine, 1950's-style diner in what I call "The Deep North Hills" of Pittsburgh. Having to take a major highway to a county road to another county road lends a wandering feel to such trips; passing signs for deer processing and taxidermy services cements that in my mind. Because Pittsburgh sits at the junction of three rivers and in the depths of a large valley, the sky seems very big near the city; further away from the city, your view is limited by hills and S-curves on the highways, and you can only see as far as the next hill, which is always very close. It's amidst one of these sets of hills that the diner is tucked away, between a few strip malls and bulletin boards advertising injury lawyers, DUI mediation and biblical messages. There are also signs pointing to more obscure roads, so that people can find biker bars, family-owned bakeries and towing services. The unofficial slogan of Pittsburgh is "You Can't Get There From Here", and this foray into the deep North Hills illustrates that, because I pass up the diner once, and then again, with my GPS's robot voice seeming to become more frustrated by the minute. I finally "see" the diner, and run in, out of breath and embarrassed, but Angela's relaxed manner disarms my anxiety, and we settle in.

Angela Gross is a strawberry-blonde, lean and athletic who speaks fast but listens hard. "I fell into the world of photography during my second pregnancy in the fall of 2009." Angela was feeling increasingly unchallenged by her part time job as a Radiology Technician at one of the major health systems in Pittsburgh. "I wanted something fresh, something new, to challenge me. I had been taking photos of our immediate family and had gotten compliments on those, so I thought that I could take a chance on developing that talent much further. I talked to my husband Dave, prayed and thought about it, and decided to go for it." By January of 2010, Angela had launched Photography 144, and through a friend made a contact who was willing to mentor her through the birth of the business.

Angela's initial foray into the world of commercial photography had some bumps in the road, but also some great learning opportunities along the way. Angela took online courses to learn about the technical aspects of photography, such as lighting, poses, and how to develop a photography blog. "I jumped into wedding photography, but after a few crazy wedding spring and summer seasons, realized that wedding photography didn't suit a balanced home life." Wedding photography, as it turns out, requires many hours of meeting with clients, forming a photographic plan (visiting the venues ahead of time, figuring out where to place lighting, etc.), and then a whole day for shoots. It is exhausting, time-consuming, and sometimes not cost-effective when you have small children at home who need their parents: both of whom need to be present to make wedding photography happen! "I decided that doing pregnancy, newborn, holiday, engagement, and senior photos and family shoots were way more conducive to stability for my family, than wedding shoots could ever be. Now I only do weddings for close friends and families who specially request them. I coordinate the other photo shoots to fit into my family schedule, and that has helped to create balance in our lives."

Dave, Angela's husband, has been an emotional and practical lifeline for her. He has given her advice, listened to her, been patient as her new work schedule and routine sometimes disrupted their family life, and has helped to critique photo shoots to present the best photo proofs to clients. As Angela started out, most of the decisions to be made had to do with how to effectively market her new business. Dave encouraged Angela to offer free senior photo sessions and photo CD's to several of the teenagers that she had met through volunteering with her daughter's Catholic school's musical troupe. "Initially, the business part of that didn't go very well, because I had an older computer and memory storage, and it was difficult to work with the new photography programs with my ancient computer equipment. Now we revamp that part of the business every year, streamlining it even more, and investing in the technical part of the business has paid for itself. The time that I have gained (from not having to slog through photo shoots using a slow computer) is priceless!"

"As far as clients go, the busier I am, and the more my name gets out there, the more ability I have to turn down clients or projects that don't appeal to me. It has become more about the creative process and helping the client to show their best selves to the camera, and less about multitasking and having anxiety about leaving my family, or pleasing the client." The more a photographer "unclenches", the more likely she is to create her best work, and therefore, to get even more clients by word of mouth. It's a creative Catch-22 that some photographers never recognize, but Angela's work beautifully demonstrates.

Angela attributes the development of her craft to three things: Dave's support and understanding, the advice of an early mentor who helped her find the right photography programs (and helped her to develop her "eye" for finding the right photos to present to clients), and believing that her Christian faith could help to form a successful business approach. "If I try to see - and photograph - the light that I see in people, and if I carefully convey the vulnerability as I find it behind the camera, that comes through in the photos. It is challenging and rewarding work, and I feel blessed and privileged by the process."

Angela also uses her Christian values to form her approaches to customer service and relationships with her clients. She believes in a transparent and honest process, and follows through with anything she promises to a client.

"On a technical angle, I also took the time to shoot photos in my "spare" time, to further develop my understanding of angle, light, and other aspects of photography. I had to learn how to self-critique when examining my own photos, because when you take hundreds of photos on a shoot, you can't overwhelm a client by showing them every single one. In the early days of my business, I often had Dave assist me in narrowing down the best photos; but taking responsibility for that aspect of the business was important to me. I also had some other photographers view my photos and give me their feedback, so that I could improve my process and proofs."

By the end of 2013, Angela had comfortably found her photography niche, also her work/life balance. Many photographers find it difficult to find the right balance between what to give their clients vs. their families vs. themselves, in time, energy, and attention (Richardson, 2014). Being a successful photographer doesn't just involve equipment and creativity; it also requires that you are "on" for the clients, every minute that you are in their presence. You are pouring your emotional, intellectual and creative energy into the process; and then when you go home, you may be pouring more emotional, mental, and creative energy into your family; what's left for yourself?

Angela has established a regular routine of working out to provide stress relief, provide self-care, and keep her mind and body in shape. She finds that challenging her body in various ways has created strength and self-discipline, but also that she has stress relief on a pretty consistent basis.

Angela has also increased her confidence and creative power by giving herself pep talks! "I find that there is something to be said for internal positive self-talk. I am in control over whether my attitude about a certain task or project takes a positive or negative tone; and even making mistakes can create space for doing the same thing better - next time."

Angela has experienced great satisfaction in using her creative gifts to preserve moments in time for her clients. Additionally, she has found that photography has blossomed other creative pursuits, such as blogging. Angela feels that she has developed a creative conscience (ie: being aware of other people's gifts, crafts, and creativity, and noticing them more) because of her pursuit of photography.

"Professionally, I feel that photography has created unexpected transferable skills, such as stress management, multitasking, being present in each moment, and discovering what inspires me and creates feelings of contentment and enjoyment. All of that growth and change has improved not only my radiology job, but my home life too."

Obviously, there are personal costs involved in adding not only a part time job, but also a small business to one's life. Before she started Photography 144, Angela had more free time to do spontaneous activities with her children and husband. She also had more flexibility in her schedule for self-care and yard work. She is more structured in how she plans, schedules, and prioritizes her time; and missing out on valuable family time has Angela rethinking her radiology tech job. In the future, she plans to quit that job and split the time gained between her family and the photography business. "I need to sit down with Dave and make a financial plan regarding losing income from my rad tech job, mostly because photography has both busy and lax seasons. I have moments of doubt about the plan, usually when the business slows down and financially - there is an impact. I do have a small business mentor who has been very encouraging and has helped to keep me going, but photography is so cyclical, it makes me nervous to take away that steady (and predictable!) income." Angela would also need to negotiate with her mother about the change in her childcare schedule, to make sure that the changes wouldn't overburden her parents.

Angela's advice to other creative types? "If you are the main breadwinner, consider your family's needs first. You need money to provide for them, and many small businesses don't succeed the first time around. If you aren't: pursue your dreams! Pursuing creative energy creates both fulfillment and drive, and those are both good things. If you find that fulfilling the dream is both possible and probable, you will have to ignore naysayers, or find practical ways to address any concerns about your plan. Not everyone is going to support such a huge life change, and that's okay. Maybe you will have to be more selective with whom you share your business plans."

Finally, Angela advises that you develop a relationship with a mentor who has already gone through the process of turning a creative pursuit into a business. "Find somebody you can trust, who will encourage you and invest time in giving you creative criticism. Having someone come alongside you will give you confidence, and help to relieve your fear and anxiety."

Michelle Gorring: Corporate Budgets vs Helping People

Michelle Gorring's home is situated in a middleclass community about 15 minutes from downtown Pittsburgh. Most houses are dual-income (quiet during the day) and the street design doesn't lend itself to neighbor "mixing", at least in the front yards. There are few sidewalks, and the streets wind around hillsides and past drop offs into valleys. The homes are situated so that their front yards are at an angle to the street, and the backyards all face each other in a shared-space design. Michelle's hospitality more than makes up for the awkward parking situation, and she welcomes me into her home with a smile and an offer of hot coffee.

Michelle is deferential, shy and sweet. Baby on her hip, she pushes masses of curly hair from her face while we talk. Her baby son only lets me hold him when he's pretty much asleep; both of her young children prefer her constant company, and her kind and gentle demeanor reveals her patience and grace. Michelle's two older children are at school, and her two younger are not of school age yet, so her days are filled with the practical needs of the young ones and her afternoons with the practical and logistical needs stemming from after school activities.

For Michelle, a convergence of events compelled her to leave her previously satisfying job as a billing office manager at a senior long-term care facility (nursing home). The most significant was the arrival of a new CEO in 2007, which signaled a change in the tone of the company. The focus started to shift from quality patient care to budgets, and long-term employees and managers began to lose their jobs as changes were made. "The management level was streamlined to include the job descriptions of people who were being forcibly retired, and some people's positions were eliminated." This focus on the bottom line created a dynamic that sent the message that the remaining employees should be grateful that they had a job, and that they were expected to do more in less time, with less resources. As a natural result of this approach, stress and tension in the working environment increased, and staff satisfaction (and the quality of patient care) decreased.

Michelle entered the Disillusionment stage of Fisher's Process:

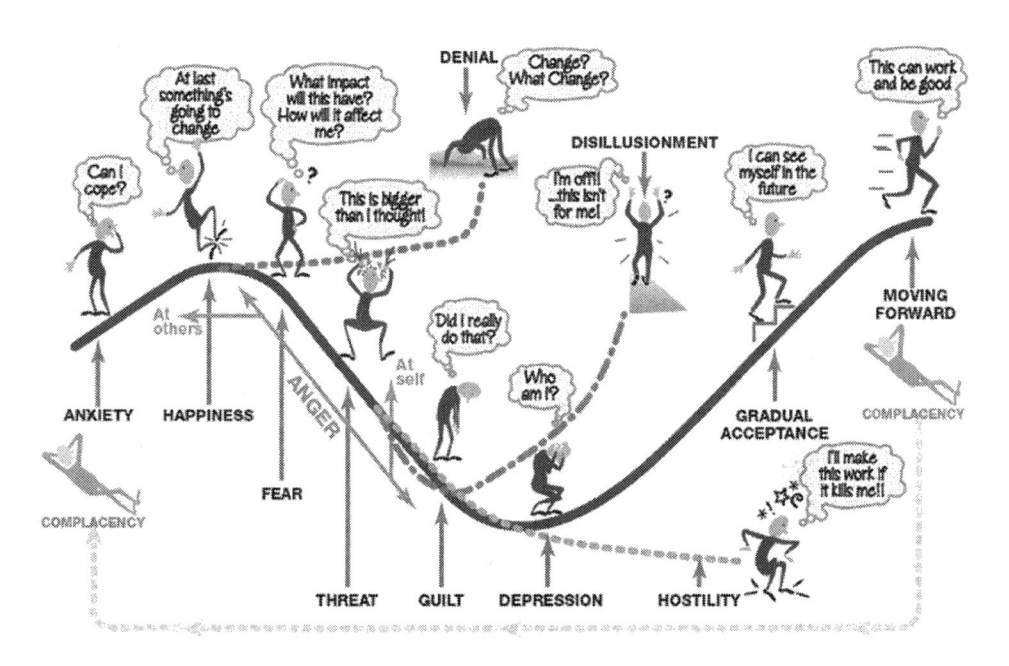

when in this stage, the employee becomes less motivated and focused, increasingly dissatisfied, and they have the feeling that they are just going through the motions. The conflict between her internal value system and the company's changed value system reached a conflict point, and she felt compelled to resign.

One of the most painful things about this experience was that Michelle had worked at the facility for 13 years, and she really enjoyed her job. After the change in CEOs, "I went home upset and stressed-out everyday"; by 2009, with a husband and two children depending on her to set the tone for home life, Michelle had some decisions before her. And sometimes, the only good reason to quit a job is because quitting is the next step to a better life (Ceniza-Levine, 2013).

As anyone who has worked in human services or healthcare knows, sometimes the salary outweighs the stress of a job, and sometimes it does not. A seemingly offhanded comment regarding an opening in staff positions by one of the employees at her children's daycare center set a new plan in motion. Michelle talked to her husband, her mother (who has been a constant emotional support), and a trusted co-worker at the nursing home before making the decision to apply to the daycare center. She knew that the position would pay a lot less than her job at the nursing home, but there were other considerations at play. Those considerations included free daycare for the children while still bringing in a salary, less travel to her job every day, and the possibility of a major decrease in stress. The daycare atmosphere was also a better fit for her personally, as it engaged her personal gifts and interests (interpersonal relations, motherly instincts, and an interest in child development).

After some internal struggle over feelings of loyalty to her work team at the nursing home, many conversations with her husband and mother, and lots of prayer to discern what she should do next, Michelle accepted the position at the daycare center and resigned her position at the nursing home. "Believe it or not, my new supervisor at the nursing home was very supportive of my decision, and was happy for me! My husband Chris was also very pleased with my decision once I started my new job, because the sense of relief over leaving my old job caused an almost immediate switch in my attitude at home. I was less stressed, and my family life improved. The relief of not having to manage people caused a noticeable increase in my positivity."

The transition to the new company was not without its complications. Her daughter was three, and didn't understand that Michelle couldn't just leave her classroom to spend time together. "I guess it was confusing to her that I was her mom, and in the same building, but couldn't leave my room every time she needed to be held or comforted." The other difficulty was getting used to the high level of energy required to deal with many children at once, for 12 hours a day, four days a week. "I left my house at six in the morning, came home six at night, and then had to come up with dinner, help my oldest with his homework, and get the laundry and dishes done. It was pretty exhausting some days!" But Michelle wholeheartedly embraced her work at the daycare center, really loved the time with the kids in her class, and was eventually promoted to lead teacher, which challenged her more and required her to be more organized in her planning.

There were also financial sacrifices in taking a job that provided less money and benefits. Her husband was being promoted from journeyman to lineman at his company, and the financial strain that was temporarily created by Michelle changing jobs meant that her mom and her husband's parents sometimes had to financially help them out. "Although we knew it was a temporary situation, the financial strain was difficult." Michelle also missed the nursing home residents and her staff team: "sometimes I would cry a little bit when I thought about them, at least at first. I also missed my solitary lunch times." And the psychological shift of going from primary to secondary breadwinner wasn't easy: "The change in roles at home was kind of messy at first; I had limited financial input, but it came with the benefit of losing all of the burden of the financial stress."

What Michelle didn't miss is the pettiness of the social politics at work, which increased significantly once the new CEO took charge in 2007. "For two years we all faced total lack of control over decisions that the new CEO made, and that affected how people treated each other. There was an decrease in how much we trusted the Human Relations department, and also, how much we trusted our coworkers."

Michelle worked at the daycare center from 2009 until 2012, when she became pregnant. She really enjoyed her time there, but with a third child on the way, it didn't make a whole lot of sense for her to continue doing 12-hour work shifts. "It was a constant juggling act between home and work obligations, so I left that job." She thinks that she will go back to work again, just not now, while her two little ones need so much love and attention (Michelle and Chris now have four children). "I will probably find a secretarial or other position at one of our district schools, so that I can have the same schedule as my kids but still make money. It will be a mental transition for me to be away from my home, but it will be less isolating for me than staying home by myself without the kids."

Michelle's advice to other mothers who are considering the same decision is "make sure that you are absolutely committed to the next job and won't have regrets." She also believes that if you are a person of faith, that you should pray about the decision and find peace about it before you make the transition, or else it won't work.

Michelle credits her easier transition to her knowledge of the center and staff beforehand, so there wasn't that uncomfortable stage where she would have had to get used to an unfamiliar environment, or making friends at a new job. She is grateful for the opportunity to have taken a step-down approach before she became a full-time stay at home mother. Michelle is now in the Moving Forward stage of Fisher's Process. She knows who she is again, is confident that she is acting in line with her personal values and convictions, and has made the right choice for herself and her family.

Chapter 5:
What Are Your Coping Skills?

There are four categories of coping skills or strategies that can be utilized during vocational transitions: appraisal-focused, problem-focused, emotion-focused, and meaning-focused (Weiten et al, 2008).

Appraisal-focused coping is directed towards challenging one's own assumptions, which could be adaptive but cognitive-based (for example, by using denial as a coping skill, or reframing techniques such as a conscious mental shift in coping approaches).

Problem-focused coping is directed towards reducing or eliminating a stressor, and could be adaptive but behavior-based (such as prevention of, or moving away from, a stressor; or, learning new skills).

Emotion-focused coping is directed towards changing one's own emotional reaction to the stressor (ie: using distraction or relaxation techniques).

Meaning-focused coping is aimed at deriving meaning from a stressful experience (for example, "What can I learn from this?").

A person can use one of these coping techniques in a job transition, or a combination of the four, or switch from one to another when they realize that one coping technique isn't working. These categories are broad enough that they encompass almost all coping skills.

Appraisal-focused coping could be described as using a "mental Rubix cube": you assess that a situation isn't being solved by a current approach, so you tweak your approach a little bit here or there until you arrive at a mental state of comfort and acceptance. An example of this type of coping is Ross Acheson (Chapter 3), who took measured cognitive steps to rework his career trajectory based on inside (not outside) forces. His mental ability to tweak his plans and paths based on changes that seemed most intuitive, point to an ability to tap into his own intrinsic values and personal directives (including his spiritual senses).

Problem-focused coping is when you encounter a vocational barrier, you either go around it, over it, or remove it altogether: a "basic training" coping technique. Think of a military recruit who is progressing through an obstacle course: you are at different times confronted with walls that you have to climb over, wooden columns to weave between, or targets that need artillery usage in order to be removed as threats. Both Poyung Lin and Feng-Chan Tsai (Chapter 3) had to "run the gauntlet" of barriers to attending American universities to progress to the next step in their vocational paths. Emily Sutton (Chapter 7) had to leave a job that provided for her (but that made her miserable) and go back to school for nursing (while working waitressing jobs) to achieve access to her true calling, her vocation. Haya Eason (Chapter 3) had to leave the military (which provided predictability and a stable income) to keep from feeling stagnant and to progress in her career. Lisa Toboz (Chapter 4) had to quit her job, pack all her belongings and put them in storage, make numerous logistical and travel decisions, and face incredulousness from loved ones in order volunteer in Croatia. This led to a better-paying job and a parallel vocation, that of a skilled photographer. There are parallels between these stories, and others: that in to GET something worthwhile, you GIVE UP something worthwhile. Taking risks is somehow intrinsically involved in problem-focused coping: many actions are required to get from one place to another, but the vocational goal wouldn't have been achieved without those action steps.

Emotion-focused coping is when you change your reactions to a vocational problem or transition to gain peace and stability. Instead of seeing the job as a problem, you change your inner attitude (feeling about work) and altitude (the idea that this problem is the "thing holding me back"). In this way, emotion-focused coping involves consistently taking responsibility for your reactions to work. Kate Grella (Chapter 4), Teresa McLaughlin (Chapter 3), and Mary Carlin* (Chapter 6) all illustrate this type of coping: given a difficult situation (whether voluntary or not), how do you change your perceptions, responses and emotions to make the most of a difficult transition? All three women were willing to take personal ownership of difficult work situations, and somehow (with support, love, and a little bit of luck) make the most of a hard transition.

Meaning-focused coping is how you take a difficult work situation, and through perspective and self-reflection, decide what you are supposed to learn from it. Mike Ryan* (Chapter 6) decided that experiencing failure in the attempt at a new vocational experience provided both trials and triumphs in areas of vocational discernment, financial investment in higher education, and navigating through relational difficulties in the wake of said failure. Stacie Schearer (Chapter 6) faced a horrific domestic abuse situation which triggered a job loss, uprooting her family, and financial problems, but took the necessary steps to learn from her experiences. Her experience included succeeding in her own personal mental health and vocational recovery. Amy Smith* (Chapter 6) decided to glean existential meaning from a bad situation when faced with multiple medical diagnoses and the loss of her military career, and ended up more connected with her family, herself, and her new future.

Each type of coping skill has advantages to using it. Some take more mental work, some more action steps, some more quietness and discerning, and some contain more existential/ spiritual work. Discerning what your preferred coping skill is and what the circumstance of the vocational problem is, can help you to discern which coping category you should attempt first.

Because mental capabilities are flexible into late adulthood, we can learn new coping skills over time by either mimicking those whom we admire, or by doing research into new types of coping and trying them out at each new vocational transition.

One thing is for certain: humans tend to repeat the same negative coping skills over and over, if new positive coping skills aren't learned and then practiced and employed. We are - at the end of the day - creatures of habit. Breaking negative coping skills requires that we learn new, positive coping skills to put in their place, which brings us to B.F. Skinner and his Operant Conditioning Theory.

Chapter 6:
Traumas that Create Crossroads

B.F. Skinner and Operant Conditioning Theory

    B.F. Skinner studied the roles of aversion, avoidance and anxiety in people's lives, and found that people will continue to respond to negative or positive input in the same way as they did the last time that something happened in their life (Skinner, 1953). He believed that human behavior becomes undeniably predictable over the course of a lifetime, especially in response to negative stimuli. Skinner believed that negative behavior creates the same responses every time (ie: the snake eating its own tail analogy), and that positive behavior creates the same responses every time. Some of his research was based on experiments using animals as subjects, examining how they responded when given either negative consequences or positive rewards (such as withdrawal of, or increase in, food).

I believe that this theory holds true *when a person's personality and coping skills remain static over the course of a lifetime.* Even if personal health declines over time, if family or other support increases conversely, responses to stress will change over the course of a person's lifetime. Amy Smith is a good example of this dynamic:

Amy Smith*: My Own Body Waged War Against Me

Amy Smith* meets me in a family-owned Italian restaurant in a Pittsburgh suburb. Laughter, the sound of televised football games, and chatter all greet me as I open the front door and find a short line of people waiting for tables. Amy arrives a few minutes later and I wave her over to our more secluded booth near the front window.

Amy is short in stature, and moves slowly across the restaurant. She has dark brown hair, but I can't see what color her eyes are, as she concentrates her gaze on the table more than she meets my eyes. Even as a casual observer, I can tell that she is in pain. She is cautious, even suspicious at first, as we have never met before; but also, because her vocational loss story is so recent and so personal. I had been told that she had a military background, so I spend the first ten minutes of her interview explaining the process and purpose of the book, share with her my husband's military history with the Navy and Army National Guard, and the brief military histories of my father and brother. She appears to relax as I reveal more of myself, and then we begin.

Amy had enjoyed a successful and exciting career in the U.S. Navy for over seven years when her health suddenly plummeted. "I was trained as a cryptographer and electrical technician in the Navy, traveled the world and enjoyed a challenging career that seemed as if it would just keep climbing. And then almost overnight, I went from complete health" to a series of baffling, mounting medical issues and tests. By the time she was honorably discharged in August of 2008, she had been diagnosed with lupus, fibromyalgia, arthritis and depression. Because of her medical issues and disabling pain, Amy went from being a completely independent career woman to working and living with relatives, and fully experiencing the Hostility phase of Fisher's Process of Transition.

Amy's friends helped her to pack up her belongings at her Navy base overseas, and Amy headed to Pittsburgh, Pennsylvania to live with her sister. "I tried to find a new normal, and first worked as a waitress and then when I couldn't maintain a full-time position at the restaurant, became a daycare provider for my sister's kids." She eventually reached out to the Veterans Administration, which steered her towards the Office of Vocational Rehabilitation. Through O.V.R. programs, she was trained to be a peer specialist in Mental Health services, and achieved her certification for that position in the fall of 2010.

Amy, age 38, is currently employed part-time as a peer specialist, has achieved her Associate's Degree and is working on her bachelor's degree, slowly but surely. She continues to financially struggle, and currently shares an apartment with her mother as she works her way towards independence. "Because of my ongoing medical issues, I may not ever be able to work full time, but financially I am working towards Social Security Disability status." One of her regrets is not preparing financially for the future while she was still in the military, which is a common complaint among military personnel who transition to civilian life (LaPonsie, 2016). Amy is working through the Gradual Acceptance stage of Fisher's Process, and as such, is actively trying to make the most of a very difficult situation.

Amy never could have anticipated that she would have lost so much, in such a short time. She misses the structure, the camaraderie, and the excitement of military life. "I also miss having good health, waking up in the morning and looking forward to the day, and not being in pain all the time." She also misses having full vocational capability and skills, and the self-mastery that comes along with career progress. But Amy's spirit remains strong, and her drive to make something of her new life is impressive. She keeps in touch with a couple of her friends in the military and is close with her family in Pittsburgh. She has a friend that she made online who encourages her to let go of her previous notions of "success," and has been a big emotional support to Amy as she grieves her former vocational aspirations and a certain future.

What has Amy gained in spite of her vocational losses? A new sense of self, simple living concepts and frugal living interests such as food canning and dehydration, holistic medicines and natural oils. "Recently I have become interested in the new trend of Small Houses, which is intriguing to me" as a viable personal investment if she is able to get Social Security Disability. As she talks about finding a small piece of land in a rural area and having a Tiny House (a dwelling structure of less than 500 square feet) built upon it, a look of peace and delight rests on her. Amy is aware and accepting of the possibility that she may live alone for the rest of her life, and accommodates her plans to this reality.

She hasn't given up, and indeed, is finding a level of peace in this life that she would never have chosen for herself. Amy has found contentment.

Donna Tarkett: Work As A Tool For Healing The Psyche

Donna Tarkett greets me at the local Eat'n Park with a smile and a hug. She is a little bit taller than me and pretty, covered in beautiful tattoos and sporting a full head of blonde dreadlocks. We grew up together in a neighboring small town, but I have only seen her a few times since her family moved when she was 16. We have both been physically transformed into softer versions of our teenage selves because childbearing, age and self-acceptance. Donna has a patient and kind demeanor, and a confident conversational style, which guides the cadence and tone of our interview.

In 2011, Donna Tarkett's partner, Jamie, died after a two-year roller coaster ride of cancer, surgery, remission and recurrence of her lung cancer. They had one adopted child, James, together, and three older children by Donna's previous marriage. For the first time in 13 years - since the start of her relationship with Jamie - Donna was facing parenting, grieving, coping, and financially providing for her family as a single person. Donna experienced the Anxiety phase of Fisher's Process:

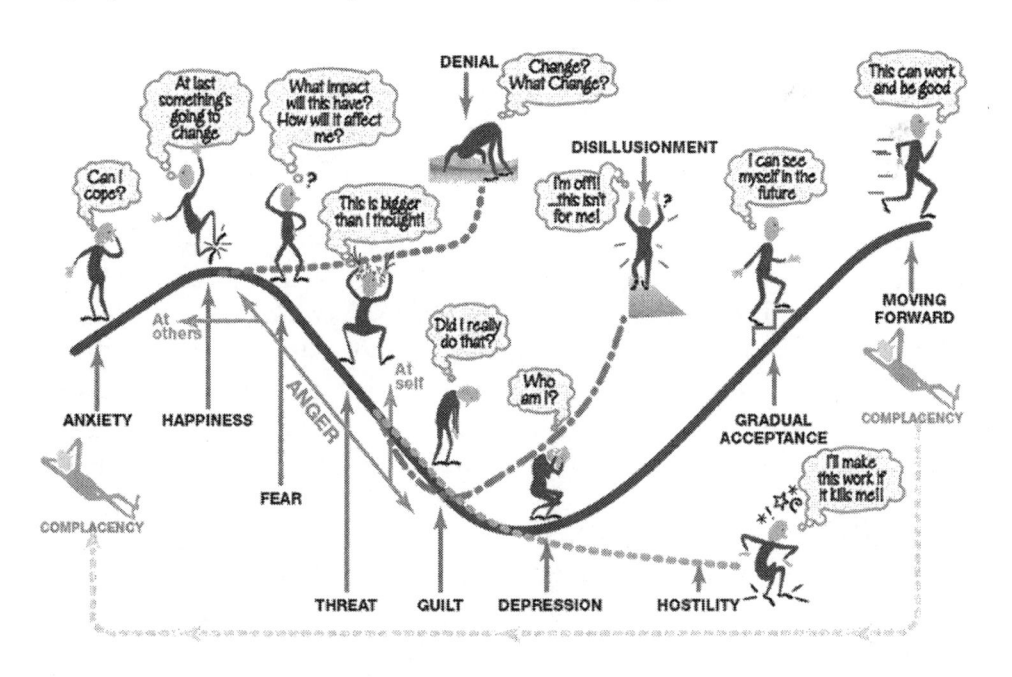

Donna was provided with a little financial breathing room after Jamie's death, thanks to a GoFundMe fundraiser that was facilitated by Donna's friends and family, "my tribe" as she refers to them. "But because there was no legal recognition of my relationship with Jamie - at the time, Pennsylvania had not legalized gay marriage - I received no death benefits, no Social Security spousal benefits, no life insurance after her death. The short respite that the GoFundMe provided my family was great, but wasn't a long-term answer to financial provision for me and my four children."

At the time of Jamie's death, Donna found a part-time job as a house cleaner. The salary wasn't lucrative enough for Donna to completely provide for her family, but it was a job that was flexible with her schedule and she already knew some of the employees. On the side, Donna began her job hunting in earnest, and decided to continue to pursue her degree.

For ten years, Donna had sporadically attended the Community College of Allegheny County in Pittsburgh, Pennsylvania. She had taken a class here, a class there, and when Donna realized that being a single parent and provider in a metropolitan area practically demanded a college degree, she decided to apply to Carlow University in Pittsburgh. Unexpectedly, the admissions counselor reported that all of Donna's cumulative classes and credits allowed her to begin at the status of a junior at the university. "I was very surprised and relieved to learn that all of those classes added up to something concrete and useful!"

In the meantime, Donna's parents, sisters and friends became her single-parent support system. Not only had they provided emotional and logistical support during Jamie's illness and after her death, but they also periodically financially assisted her. In addition, Donna received support from individual therapy and from CoDA, a 12-step program that equips people with codependent tendencies to learn how to develop and maintain healthy relationships. One of the things that Donna had realized over the course of Jamie's illness and death was that Donna had codependent tendencies, and that she tended to look to Jamie for validation, guidance and relevance. "I didn't want to make that mistake again, and knew that it was in my hands to change that pattern of relating."

As a stay-at-home mom who had homeschooled for many years, Donna found herself in unfamiliar territory as she looked for jobs that would both provide for her family AND allow some scheduling flexibility, so that she could finish her degree and also meet the needs of her children's schedules. She was looking for a job that fit her personal philosophies and values, that would allow her to help people who were in need or disenfranchised. At times she found herself returning to Fisher's stages of Anxiety and Disillusionment.

Eventually, in 2014, Donna found the perfect fit as a Family Support Specialist at Sojourner House in Pittsburgh, Pennsylvania. Sojourner House is an organization which provides long-term intensive treatment for women with all types of substance addiction, and provides housing, counseling and support for them and their children. Donna works there as a Parent Educator, so that women can leave the program with parenting and family skills that can help them to be successful when life gets stressful outside of the support of the House. "I loved Sojourner House right away, I was philosophically ready and mentally healthy, so was excited to be in a helping profession." Donna was in the Gradual Acceptance stage of Fisher's Process, in which an employee starts to see that they are getting validation of their thoughts and actions. They are eager to manage the control of their work life, which then leads to self-confidence and self-mastery.

Donna is also effusive about her work team. "They are good people, most of them are Christian but aren't preachy about it, they do their job to help our clients, have a passion for people and desire to see them do well, as do I. We share a common goal and language in that." In the year since Donna began her job at Sojourner House, she has moved fully into the Moving Forward stage of Fisher's Process, in which an employee exerts more control over their work life, makes more things happen for themselves, and have a well-developed sense of self at work. There is a sense of coherence and cooperation between personal values and work values.

The largest adjustment, the most growing pains, as Donna has become acclimated to being sole provider for her family, has been keeping a grip on the many needs of a home and four children! "I came to realize that it's pretty much impossible to work full-time AND to keep my house in order, so I'm just trying to keep on top of things as best I can." Her oldest daughter, who is 23, has recently moved out of state; and her son, who is 16, now lives with his father in a neighboring town so that he can attend the school of his choice and be raised by his dad. Although the size of Donna's "tribe" has shrunk a little, she has a new(ish) relationship with her live-in boyfriend of two years, a new lease on life, her son James is doing well in school, and life is…full! Donna shares many common interests with her boyfriend, including landscaping their urban backyard, raising chickens, and playing in a local band.

Donna misses a lot of things about being a stay-at-home mom. She misses the constant interaction of homeschooling and taking care of her growing kids 24/7, being the biggest influence on them without the added stress of the outside world and a job, the spontaneity of a stay-at-home day, and keeping her home the way she did when her home was her full-time job. Their whole family is now a "slave to the clock: what time to get up for work, get my kids off to their various places, and fit in grocery shopping, errands, etc. around my job."

As Donna (now age 45) continues with her university education, she realized that she has come into her own since Jamie's death, but it hasn't always been easy to do. "Work helped me to get through the grief, but each of us in the family coped differently with her death; we each went off to our own 'coping corners' and we still tend to retreat to them when things are stressful. When I finish my bachelor's degree, I will go to working on my master's degree at Carlow, because I need that in order to be a counselor or therapist for kids. I would like to work at a school or organization in which I help homeless, at-risk and disenfranchised children." Children get hurt the worst when adults' decisions go badly, and Donna is determined to become a professional who can help in such situations.

There are some things Donna would do differently if she could go back: she wouldn't date right away, nor jump right into a job out of a sense of anxiety. "On the one hand, starting work right away distracted me, and helped me to grieve over time. On the other hand, maybe I was sometimes more distracted than my kids needed me to be? But I can't regret where I am, because I am in a really good place right now, and so are my kids."

"I would suggest that you be in your grief and deal with it, don't jump into something else right away, including dating. My kids deserved my full attention, and they didn't really have it."

Jack Watson: ...And Never The 'Twain Shall Meet

I meet with Jack Watson in his retirement community's conference room, a small and sparsely-furnished space that Jack seems to fill up with his imposing stature and strong voice. He is tall and broad-shouldered, his military bearing holding on even into his '90's. His firm handshake accompanies a few quick questions about the intent and trajectory of my book project. He is curious, intelligent, practical and respectful. I think, "This is what my husband will be like in 50 years." It was an interesting glimpse into the (possible) future, and his story grabs my attention right away.

Jack Watson's transition from military to civilian life felt more like a door slammed and then nailed shut: coming back from World War II and transitioning to civilian life was not easy, but "American society had an unspoken understanding: come back from war, get back to life, and chalk it all up to life experience." And considering the traumatizing experiences that Jack had on the island of Iwo Jima, Japan, he was more than happy to do just that.

Jack's path to Iwo Jima started with a strong sense of responsibility to his country; after only two months in college at Penn State in Pennsylvania, he decided to join the war effort by volunteering for the Marines. He was assigned to the 4th Marine Division, which was one of the most active groups of soldiers in the Pacific arena during the war. "Eventually my Division landed on Iwo Jima, a Japanese island that was heavily guarded by Japanese troops but was considered vital to the Allies, as it was needed as a stopping point for planes that had exhausted their fuel and other reserves while bombing Japan."

On February 19, 1945, Allied troops, including the 4th Division of the U.S. Marines, descended on Iwo Jima and the next 30 days were some of the bloodiest of World War II. Jack Watson was right in the thick of it.

"As a sergeant, day after day I sent groups of men into battle, engaging the enemy and trying to gain ground. Every evening we had to fall back in order to allow for a buffer zone between our Marines and the Japanese, which lost us ground and cost the 4th Division valuable human lives."

Jack's frustration grew each day, as did his exhaustion. As a sergeant, he had to follow orders, whether he personally felt that his men were losing ground every day, or that they were so exhausted that they just couldn't engage the Japanese for another 12 hours, or another, or another....

Jack and his men also had to contend with the surreal atmosphere. The smell of sulfur and decomposing bodies ("try as we might, we were never able to bury as many bodies as we needed to during evening hours"), the heat, the hunger and thirst, the tension, and the psychological assault sometimes felt too much for anyone to bear. That was true for the Japanese soldiers as well, as Jack discovered when he experienced a bizarre exchange with a Japanese soldier, face-to-face. The American and Japanese troops had been fighting against each other all day, and Jack's troops were fighting in hand-to-hand combat with the Japanese: "There were bodies from both sides all over the ground, dead and wounded men piling up."

Jack became so physically, mentally, and spiritually exhausted that he could barely raise his head, and he prayed to God to spare his life. "I sensed someone behind me, and slowly turned around. A Japanese soldier was standing there, close enough for me to look him straight in the eyes." What he saw there still haunts him to this day: a mirror image of himself: exhaustion, fear, a weariness from the war. The men both turned around and walked away.

On March 19, 1945 the Allied forces finally defeated the Japanese on Iwo Jima, and by 1946 Jack Watson had returned to the States. Through the G.I. Bill, Jack attended Penn State University for free and he also received a monthly living allotment. "I reconnected with friends, many of whom had returned from war with a similar desire to put those experiences behind them and to get on with their lives." During this time Jack was very busy and moved quickly through the Depression, Gradual Acceptance, and Moving Forward stages of Fisher's Process. "I used physical activity, my intellect, and socializing to distract myself from any negative feelings about the war."

Having an active social life positively impacted Jack's transition from military to civilian life. Jack's brother was dating a woman whose best friend, Helen, was attending Slippery Rock University, and the two couples often went out together. Jack's new girlfriend (who eventually became his wife) and his college classes kept Jack busy. Also, "I am a Christian, and my faith really helped me through the transition from wartime to peacetime." Jack had strong support from his future wife, his college friends, and his siblings. He rarely discussed his wartime experiences, and did what most World War II veterans did: they got back from the war and got busy living life; however, "many soldiers came back with alcohol problems, and had serious issues trying to maintain normal family and work lives."

The main coping skills that Jack used to transition from the military to civilian life were a sense of purpose and activity that centered around college, his social life and new romance, but also a determination to put the past behind him and to invest energy into his faith life.

Now age 92, Jack Watson has had a fulfilling family life and a career in business. It may be the very intensity of his wartime experiences that moved him quickly through the stages of Depression and Gradual Acceptance, and into Moving Forward.

Sometime in the last decade, Jack decided to write down his wartime experiences, and allowed his wife to read his musings. Her reflection on his recollection was this: "Jack, you wrote down what you did and what you saw and what happened, but not how you <u>felt</u> about all of it." Jack is still considering it.

Mary Carlin: Between Space and Time*

Mary Carlin* and I meet at her suburban home in the South Hills of Pittsburgh. Her back yard is small but cozy; trees surround a patio space that includes a small above ground pool and a patio. She asks her older son to keep her mother and her sister company while we talk outside; her younger son puts on sunglasses and floats in the pool, wandering in and out to get snacks or to use the bathroom.

Mary is soft-spoken and mild-mannered. She looks younger than her 50 years, smiles often and is encouraging and complimentary in her speech. Mary's intention is to speak about her transition from the work world to becoming a stay at home mom, but the conversation meanders to her current vocation, which is caretaker to her elderly mother Betty* and her sister Jen*, who has multiple sclerosis and is bipolar. Jen is wheelchair bound, and requires 24-hour assistance and care. Between Mary, her children, Ben* (her husband), and a caretaker who comes to the house to help with Jen's care, it is a coherent melding of compassion, mercy and cooperation.

"In 2002, Ben had just been laid off from his job, which was alarming because he was the sole financial provider for our family (our two boys were one and five years old at the time). Three things happened at once: Ben lost his job, my mother had started to have some difficulty caring for her home, and my sister's multiple sclerosis started to worsen." Jen could no longer care for herself, but Mary couldn't see committing her to a personal care home or treatment facility.

Mary and her husband Ben made the decision to meet with her mom and make a proposal: if Mary and Ben could move into Betty's home with their two boys, Ben would look for work in that area and maintain the house. "That would allow my mom and sister to stay in their home. It would also mean that my mom would get to watch her grandchildren grow up." Ben and Mary also agreed to pay for any improvements that were necessary to accommodate Jen's disability. Betty agreed to the terms, and so Mary and Ben moved their family from Avalon, PA, into Betty's home in the South Hills of Pittsburgh.

At first, the adjustment to moving back into her childhood home was stressful and a little strange. Betty had very strong opinions as to Mary and Jen's "place" in her home, and it was difficult for the siblings to be able to express their opinions about how the cooperative home would function. "I felt like her 'kid' moving back in, like I wasn't being treated like an adult who had an equal stake in how the house would run. It felt like stepping backwards in time." Mary says that if she could do it all over again, she would never have suggested to Ben this whole arrangement. She is in the Depression Stage of Fisher's Process; she feels stuck in her decision, and is trying to make the best of the situation. It is simply not an option to quit her "job" here; caretaking has become her default vocation.

Because of Mary's significant caretaking and family obligations that resulted from their 2002 move, her husband has turned down exciting and lucrative jobs in other towns and Mary herself has experienced a considerable constriction in her lifestyle that she did not anticipate. "Unless Jen's caretaker is available, I have no ability to even leave the house for more than an hour. My sons are very helpful, but it is not feasible to leave teenagers to care for a severely handicapped adult."

According to the Office on Women's Health, a division of the U.S. Department of Health and Human Services, caregiver stress manifests itself through these symptoms:
Feeling overwhelmed
Feeling alone, isolated, or deserted by others
Sleeping too much or too little
Gaining or losing weight (significant amount)
Feeling tired most of the time
Losing interest in activities you used to enjoy
Becoming easily irritated or angered
Feeling worried or sad often
Having frequent headaches or body aches

Women who care for loved ones who need constant care and supervision are especially prone to serious health problems, putting them at risk for depression and anxiety; weakened immune systems;

obesity; chronic diseases such as heart disease, cancer, arthritis and diabetes; and problems with short-term memory and focus (Link & Hepburn, 2015).

So it's not just the physical work that Mary is doing with Jen that can be harmful (bathing her, changing her clothes and bedding, doing excess laundry), but the emotional strain (always being verbally positive in order to be supportive of her sister, curbing her tongue, subsuming her personal desires in order to meet the needs of her sister and mother), the mental overload (scheduling and arranging transportation to various medical appointments, scheduling the caregiver's shifts, arranging payments for the various support services that Jen receives, tracking insurance payments, being a medical advocate for her sister) and the significant work she does as a stay at home mom (schedules for all six family members, cleaning a multi-level house, cooking meals, doing laundry, making time accommodations to balance out Ben's long commute to work).

Mary's mom Betty has significantly declined in physical strength and mental acuity since the two households merged in 2002. Betty is physically frail and had to stop driving at the age of 90, because her physical responses aren't quick enough to safely drive anymore. She is not financially savvy, and could be taken advantage of if she were living alone. Additionally, Betty is experiencing some cognitive delays in the areas of medication management and self-care (showering, dressing, etc.). "Intellectually, she isn't as sharp as she used to be, and it is hard for me to have complicated conversations with her, so she isn't the same kind of companion that she used to be."

Mary's sister Jen has also significantly (and alarmingly) physically declined in the last few years. She is completely immobilized and needs constant care and supervision, and Mary plays a large part in her daily care. "It has been so difficult watching Jen decompensate over these past 14 years that we have lived together, watching my sister's personality retreat further and further into the shell that her body has become." Mary didn't truly appreciate the ongoing decline until it was happening and she acknowledged it. It is like losing her sister, like watching her die, but it's taking years and years.

There are other losses associated with being a caretaker that Mary feels deeply: "I have a lack of freedom in my schedule, my personal space, my marital privacy (where do we have arguments without being overheard by my mom and sister?), my parenting (input by my mom), and my ability to change decor in the house when I so desire."

     Mary initially had plans to go back to work in Interior Design once her children were both in school, but those plans were derailed when Mary realized that keeping Jen and Betty out of nursing homes necessitated that she abandon plans for her ideal career. That being said: "I have freely chosen this path, no one bullied me into it, and I feel that I made that decision based on the needs of the rest of the family." Mary's husband Ben is very supportive, giving her assistance with practical tasks, but he is also good about helping her to see when she is getting burned out and is not taking care of herself. Ben has also helped Mary to become more assertive and sure of herself, encouraging her to have good boundaries with her family, and to explicitly ask for personal space. That has helped Betty, especially, to become less controlling with house issues and details.

     One of the other losses amidst this arrangement is normative family dynamics: "There is no spontaneity in our family life. Being sensitive to Jen's caretaker's schedule, I can't just up and decide to go for a date night, or to spontaneously go with Ben and the kids somewhere. Everything is carefully scheduled, orchestrated and planned. Now that my mom and sister have higher needs, I feel guilty about the cost that my husband and children have paid so that I can do this for my mom and sister."

     Sometime in the future, Mary would like to work for a school or parish, something that wouldn't be an all-consuming career. That will only happen if or when she is no longer a caretaker.

     Mary has been sustained by support and understanding from her husband and her sons, but also from a friend who has taken care of her own mom. Mary also gains great comfort from her Catholic faith and belief system, and her eternal perspective: "I have recently become even more peaceful, come to a better place, about my service to my family. I have become aware that having gratitude about the 'little' things, like being physically able to do my caretaking duties, having a husband with a good job, and having two wonderful, helpful sons, that is the silver lining." Mary specifically prays that her gratitude will continue to increase, and that she will have peace and patience with the long road ahead of her. As far as self-care, she attempts to go to a local community center for exercise a few times a week. She also copes with uncomfortable and awkward moments at home by finding the humor in them. Mary is now in the Gradual Acceptance Phase.

Mary's advice to other potential/new caretakers is this: "Set up boundaries, right away. Be specific about what you are willing (or able) to do. If possible, set defined rules around what is expected from you, from your family member, so that you don't feel like the expectations are always changing. Also, help to set up future medical and care plans for your family member. Know about their values around money, medical care, whether they want a Do Not Resuscitate medical order, etc. Details are important! And knowing their wishes ahead of time will give you some peace."

Frank Stuparitz: The Death of the Old Dream Meant My Survival

Frank Stuparitz is a former Pittsburgher who is now living in Florida, so our interview is by phone; not my favorite arrangement, but the mutual friend who referred him to me assures me that Frank's story is unique, captivating and worth adjusting my protocol. I am pleasantly surprised by the experience.

Semi-retired physical therapist Frank Stuparitz, age 67, seems at first to be a fairly typical person. With three grown children, a devoted wife, and retirement plans in the works, hearing his whole vocational transformation story surely catches a person unawares.

"I don't miss anything about being a priest," Frank Stuparitz says, "So many people expect you to be 'their' priest (whatever that might mean), and people see your collar, but they don't see you as a whole person."

"I see now that I never really was supposed to be a priest; I remember being a teenager and thinking that maybe I should consider it, but there was never a strong personal draw towards the priesthood, no concrete conviction." He began seminary classes while still in high school, continued after graduation, achieved his bachelor's degree in Philosophy, and a master's in Divinity. Frank was ordained and then placed in his first parish in 1973 and stayed there for five years. He was then moved to a second parish; conflicts arose between him and that pastor, and unresolved stress and anger over those conflicts resulted in mild back pain. Over the next five years, Frank was an effective priest, using his administrative and pastoring skills, but the back pain increased in intensity and frequency. He was treated along the way by various physical therapists, but only found temporary alleviation of the chronic pain. He was in the Denial stage of Fisher's Transition Process.

Being the oldest of six children, Frank felt a heightened sense of responsibility to continue in the priesthood. However, he realized that his physical pain was being caused by an internal conflict between what he felt <u>obligated</u> to be, and who his true self might be. He sought counseling from a therapist whom he was referred to, who was a laicized former priest. During this time, Frank moved into the Disillusionment stage of Fisher's Transition Process:

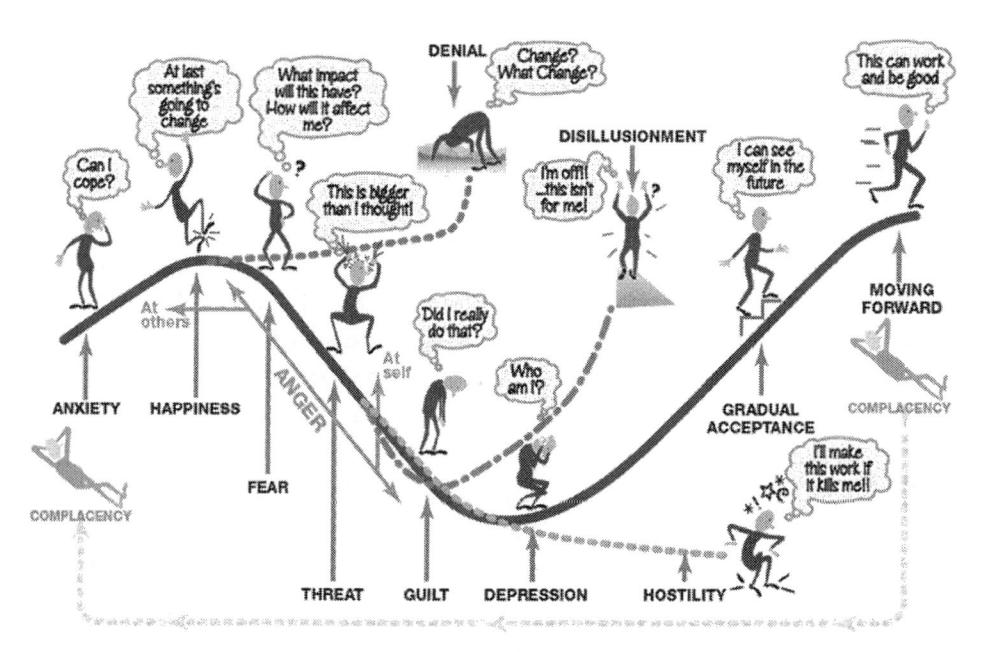

![Fisher's Transition Process diagram showing stages: Anxiety, Happiness, Fear, Threat, Guilt, Depression, Hostility, Gradual Acceptance, Moving Forward, Complacency, with Denial and Disillusionment peaks, including thought bubbles such as "Can I cope?", "At last something's going to change", "What impact will this have? How will it affect me?", "This is bigger than I thought!", "Change? What Change?", "Did I really do that?", "Who am I?", "I'm off! ...this isn't for me!", "I can see myself in the future", "This can work and be good", and "I'll make this work if it kills me!"]

"I decided to take a leave of absence to discern whether to continue on the path of priesthood. I worked with my counselor on various issues regarding personal plans, my faith life, and my future. The counselor was very good about not letting me blame-shift, not putting the responsibility for the decision on anyone else besides myself." Immediately upon beginning his leave of absence, Frank felt a weight being lifted from him; this feeling was accompanied by a realization that his parents and friends had their own ideas about his future, and wouldn't realize that he was leaving the priesthood until a true separation from the vocation occurred. During this time, Frank was experiencing the Hostility phase of Fisher's Process.

Frank notified the office of his diocese in 1983 that he intended to permanently separate himself from the vocation, and spent some time that year in solitude and meditation. He had to move back in with his parents for a year or so, and spent time with his youngest brother, who was twenty years younger than himself and was a support to Frank, as was Frank's counselor, his parents, and four priest friends. There were some uncomfortable feelings within the extended family, as Frank's uncle was also a priest and there was some tension around Frank's decision to leave the priesthood. Frank formally started the process of laicization (the process of the loss of the clerical state: Caridi, 2009) in 1988, and he received word of its completion in 1996.

Frank worked for a limo service for a few years; during that time he met and married his wife, who had an eight-year-old daughter. "We then had a daughter together in 1985, the same year that I lost my job with the limo service, in the same week that I opened the newspaper and saw two full pages of available physical therapy jobs." He decided to go to PT school and until he graduated from college in 1990, worked a variety of jobs that would fit in with his class schedule and home life, including school bus driving, lawn care, and care of adults with mental retardation. During this time, Frank and his wife had a third child, and tried to maintain a balance of work, home, and school life. Frank had progressed to the Moving Forward stage of Fisher's Process.

For more than 25 years, Frank has worked in the field of physical therapy, in both intensive inpatient and acute rehabilitation settings. Frank really enjoys his career, and finds great satisfaction in helping people, and in watching their rehabilitation progress. Last year, he and his wife moved to Florida to be close to his daughter and her significant other: "he has multiple sclerosis and can't walk, so we moved in to help him out and support them both."

Frank's new job in Florida is more intense, and he feels more pressure to be computer savvy. He plans to work full-time for two more years, and then another couple of years part-time, and then retire when he is 71 or 72.

Frank never regretted his decision to leave the priesthood, and believes that he would have only become debilitated by pain and anger if he had stayed. He would encourage others who are considering a drastic vocational change to surround themselves with people who will allow them to speak freely and honestly; to find a few people who will encourage challenging opportunities to explore life with open eyes; and to NOT stay under the radar like he did. "The beginning of my mistakes was wandering into the priesthood instead of challenging myself to figure out where I was supposed to be; instead I went where I was expected to be."

Rosie C*: Losing A Third of Her Family Circle

Rosie C.*, age 43, attended business school after high school, and works as a paralegal in a city in the northeastern United States. She recently became a widow after her husband Dave died, from a long lasting (and secret) illness. Rosie meets with me in her suburban cottage-style home, one of her orange tabby cats gently pawing my ankle as we settle in to talk. Tall and blond with a raspy voice, she bluntly says, "So where should I start?"

During their marriage, Rosie and Dave both worked full-time to provide a comfortable home for their son Liam. But unlike many couples' financial stories, Rosie's salary was used for the family's expenses. "Regardless, Dave's salary provided our family certain luxuries, such as travel and other family experiences, that we were all grateful for."

The biggest adjustment, though, comes in the form of his absence from the house: Dave's big, opinionated and boisterous personality lent a vitality to the house that now feels like an "echo" in their home. "Our son Liam was close with Dave, and had a particularly difficult adjustment after the death of his father." Rosie not only had the task of mentally shifting into the role of sole provider and widow, but also taking on the role of single parent.

Rosie's transition in those roles has been made easier by the support of her family. "My mother provided care and company for Liam over the summer after Dave's death, and my older brother came to help me get my house in order soon after the funeral." Rosie felt a pull to make physical improvements to her home, to get organized and declutter. She knew that even if she fell into financial trouble, or required extra help with Liam, that her family would assist her in any way that she needed.

Despite the welcome assistance of loved ones, Rosie especially misses the advantage of having Dave to help her with parenting a teenage son. "Helping a child grieve while grieving the loss of your co-parent, spouse and best friend is reality for millions of Americans. According to the U.S. Census Bureau, about 15 million women ages 35 to 49 are widows; some 5 million men in the same bracket are widowers. Many also are parents of young kids." (Bluethmann, 2015). Parenting can be largely an exercise in hope and positivity, and has external actions that are usually visible. Grieving is largely an exercise in submitting your will to the universe, letting go of hopes that you had for that person and mourning any future memories with them. It is mostly an internal and invisible process. How do you reconcile the two actions and not buckle under the dichotomy? Sometimes that involves taking care of yourself <u>first</u> so that you can be revitalized to take care of your child. And sometimes, that means pursuits that are solitary but rejuvenating, like yoga.

 Rosie's next vocational transition (in addition to her current career) is her plan to become a yoga instructor. She has started the training, and hopes to eventually teach yoga part-time while also working at her current job. Yoga provided her a physical, spiritual and personal respite while she was grieving, and Rosie is eager to help others who may be experiencing similar stressors. She also leaves open the possibility of changing companies, though not careers. She is very comfortable working in patent law, and desires to stay in that field.

 Rosie's advice includes journaling to help process through grief and anger; to practice forgiveness for those who can't walk through a difficult time alongside you; to take a measured and holistic approach when in the anger and bargaining stages of grief; to be open to practices like yoga or meditation that you normally wouldn't "reach for" in a crisis; and to accept offered help when you need it.

 Rosie says: "Be kind to yourself; there is no timeline for grief, when it begins and when it ends; stay awake during the process and you will get through it to the other side."

Stacie Schearer: What Doesn't Kill You

 Stacie Schearer meets me in a local Eat'n'Park restaurant, gives me a hearty hug and plops herself down in the booth. Stacie cuts an imposing figure, blonde, buxom, and taller than me, with piercing eyes and a very direct gaze. Diners all around us talk and laugh loudly, as we also often do during her interview. Stacie and I used to work together for a mental health residential non-profit company, and we fall back into conversational rhythm as she reveals everything that has transpired since the day that she "fell off" my radar, as it were, in 2004.

 Mother's Day is meant to be a celebration, a time to pause and honor those women who care for, love, and teach their children well. But for Stacie Schearer, a survivor of domestic abuse, it is also a reminder of the worst day of her life.

 "The most violent cycle of abuse started when my husband lost his mother and was also laid off from his job in 2005. Things became so tense by the fall of 2005 that I had a hard time concentrating at work, and my performance at work was suffering." Concurrently, she was taking oxycontin to deal with chronic physical pain; her husband had "helped" her by telling her that crushing and snorting it would get it into her system faster, and Stacie had gotten addicted to the medicine. By December of 2005 her dwindling and erratic work performance resulted in a referral to the Employee Assistance Program counselor, with whom Stacie was required to have meetings.

Stacie kept the secret that she was being regularly abused at home, and that she and her husband both were abusing drugs. "The high level of stress that I was constantly trying to "manage" included keeping my girls safe at home, maintaining my job responsibilities, hiding my drug problem, and being under huge financial pressure." She took two weeks off in December of 2005, in the hopes that some time off would improve her ability to focus, but returned to work as distracted and stressed as ever.

Everything finally came to a devastating crisis in February of 2006, when her husband was arrested for stealing scrap metal. The arrest was public knowledge, and resulted in a meeting between Stacie and her employer's Human Resources Director. The Director allowed Stacie to resign so that she could collect unemployment, instead of firing her for her job performance issues, which would have financially devastated her family. With both Stacie and her husband now unemployed, under financial pressure, and at home with two small children, the stress finally exploded their family apart on Mother's Day of 2006.

On that fateful day, Stacie awoke after being unconscious for over 24 hours. Her husband had repeatedly attacked her, and then choked her into submission. By the time her husband returned to the house that day, Stacie had her older daughter take photos of the injuries, cleaned herself up, attended to her two little girls, and devised a plan: this time, the last time - she had to make a permanent move to help herself and her kids out of this volatile and life-threatening situation.

On Monday morning her husband left the house, so Stacie called the domestic abuse hotline, reported the assault and her husband's extensive drug use history. With the abuse services' coordination, it was arranged for the police to come to the house the following morning. At approximately 9 am on Tuesday morning, 15 policemen showed up at their front door. They signaled the end of seven years of a cycle of abuse, reconciliation, normalcy, and more abuse. "I was ready and willing to do whatever it would take to shield my children and myself from any more abuse and chaos, including leaving my life in Pittsburgh behind me."

Stacie's husband was arrested and taken to jail. He was processed through the system and awaited trial for attempted murder. Stacie contacted her parents, who picked up Stacie and her girls and moved them back to Stacie's hometown in northern Pennsylvania. Stacie's parents had suspected that she was being abused, and had previously travelled across the state to drop in on the family in the summer of 2005. Stacie's sister-in-law, who was a prison corrections officer, helped Stacie's parents to understand that addiction is an illness, and facilitated their understanding of the process of recovery that Stacie was about to go through.

Stacie entered intensive drug and alcohol therapy in July of 2006 near her hometown, and graduated from the program in August of 2007. In the meantime, Stacie filed for divorce and waited for her husband to come up for trial. He received more than four years as a sentence, and their divorce was finalized.

Stacie's fresh start in her hometown was tough but successful. All the reserves of strength that she had built up over a lifetime of overcoming personal obstacles, including getting married at a young age, achieving her master's degree while working full-time, and trying to live a fulfilling life while in an abusive marriage, came to bear during Stacie's addiction recovery. Stacie participated in not only substance abuse programs like Narcotics Anonymous, but domestic abuse therapy and groups. She needed a lot of support to piece back together her psyche, her self-esteem, and her physical health. She met a lovely man, Scott, in January of 2007, and they began a relationship. Stacie had extensive support from her parents and friends, and from Scott as well. Scott helped Stacie to become a high-functioning, motivated person again: "His love for me didn't do the work FOR me, but helped me to see that I was capable of it, myself." Also, Stacie's self-mastery to provide for, and be a good example to her girls, was enabled by her divorce from her ex-husband.

After two years in prison, Stacie's ex-husband came up for parole. Stacie had seen his transformation over that time, and that he was clean and sober and wanted to be a good father to his girls, and in that belief argued for early release on good behavior. The parole board refused to release him. He completed all 4.5 years of the original prison sentence.

By the beginning of 2013, Stacie was married to Scott and had decided to seek employment again in Pittsburgh. She had been laid off from her recruitment position for the energy industry in northern Pennsylvania, which created uncertainty in her life. "I was looking for a fresh perspective and a new start for my career." The severance package from her employer gave her a little breathing room while looking for work. Stacie, Scott, and her two daughters returned to Pittsburgh. Scott and Stacie began new jobs within two weeks of settling in Pittsburgh, and Stacie's younger daughter started classes at a local school.

Stacie is overqualified for many positions because of her extensive work history and degree, and many employers are reluctant to hire her in a "lower" position because of her resume. She is overhauling her resume and cover letters to resolve this.

Stacie has a lot of advice regarding similar domestic abuse situations: "Be steadfast in what is best for the family, no matter what. IF your ex-spouse or partner reforms their ways, take the tact that I did: 'Don't tell me, SHOW me that you have changed.' If the other parent becomes safe again, make every effort to co-parent, children always do better when it is possible for both parents to be involved in their lives. Facilitate communication between the kids and your ex when he/she becomes safe again. Don't give up on yourself, that's not an option when you have children involved...believe in yourself, and push through! I never knew how strong I was until all of this happened to me and my kids."

Carol Pruchnitzky: Losing Ground, Gaining Perspective

Carol Pruchnitzky welcomes me into her home, a brick cottage-style home in a hilly Pittsburgh suburb. Her diminutive stature belies her strength of character, and her ability to bounce back from great difficulty. Carol has three children, and works full-time as an office manager for an accounting firm, earning a very modest salary. Her oldest child is 28, married with one child; and her youngest child is 15. "My life was predictable and pretty happy, until two years ago when I woke up to find that my husband Michael had died of a heart attack in the middle of the night."

And so, at the young age of 49, she suddenly had to scramble to adjust to life on several different fronts: as a single mom, as sole financial provider for her family, and as a widow. Financially, the impact didn't really register until the life insurance money ran out and she had to apply for Parent Plus loans for her middle child, who was a sophomore in university. The impact is felt daily as she struggles to survive on her small salary, because she is also financially assisting a relative. The relative experienced unexpected medical expenses (and lost salary) from surgery for a brain tumor and subsequent follow-up care.

In addition to the financial impact, the social impact of being widowed has been surprising, as "many friends' support faded after the funeral was over, and people got back to their everyday lives." Carol senses that couples who were friends with her and Mike are not sure how to socially include their suddenly-single friend. She spends many weekend nights alone or with her children.

Functionally, she has struggled to adjust to being suddenly responsible for every head-of-household role: budgeting, taking care of house repairs and improvements, budgeting for normative auto expenses, buying or arranging for repairs of appliances, etc. Carol and Mike had clear delineation of household roles during their marriage, which left Carol struggling to fill the gaps that were left by Mike's death. She describes herself as having a "serious lack of budgeting and organization skills," but has no other choice but to adjust herself to her new reality.

This new life also means a shift in her view of herself as providing supplemental income to the household, and has caused her to reconsider whether her current occupation is sufficient to provide for her family. Carol is in the Depression stage of Fisher's Process. "I feel that I have no other choice but to put my resume on the market, and hope that my long history at my job will help me to find a higher-paying job." This experience has made Carol reflect on what is important, what to let go and what to fight for.

Besides the obvious - missing her husband terribly! - Carol also misses the financial security that his income provided her and the children. Carol anticipates that her three children, her daughter-in-law and her grandchild will be her biggest support as she embarks on this next chapter of her career path.

Mike Ryan: The Road Less Traveled*

Mike Ryan*, age 47, meets me at King's Restaurant on Neville Island, a riverside community that periodically experiences flooding because of being surrounded by rivers downstream of Pittsburgh. He eagerly takes me up on the offer of a pseudonym, so that he can be completely honest while telling me of his most recent vocational loss. Mike wears his heart on his sleeve, his eyes and facial expression either brightening or darkening, depending on the topic and whether he can lend humor to that part of his story. He is considerate with his words, and gently corrects any misperceptions as I reflect some of his answers.

Mike thought that finally finishing his bachelor's degree in May 2013 would set him on the path of a stable, challenging and interesting career. "After two decades as an associate engineer*, I was also looking forward to becoming a teacher, and engaging young minds" in the discipline of math concepts.

However, what began as an initial foray into the educational system soon became an exercise in frustration and a lesson in educational politics. Mike was initially wary of working with learning disabled students, and working with pre-teens and teenagers with autism and developmental disabilities was certainly a challenge. "But the more frustrating aspect of my year in the Ohio public school system was the implementation of Common Core curriculum."

The teachers at his charter school were expected to educate the students using Common Core, a new curriculum that was financially and politically backed by Bill Gates (Layton, 2014). The driving force behind Common Core is a push to nationalize (instead of maintaining state-centric) education standards, thereby preparing students to be prepared for college in a more consistent manner.

What the charter school teachers in Mike Ryan's school discovered was this: that Common Core didn't work for their disabled students; that the Common Core standards didn't account for the inappropriate same-age expectations of their students who had serious learning delays, behavioral issues and in some cases, mental health concerns. It was comparing apples to oranges, and the frustration level in the classroom (fed by the students' performance anxieties and the growing teacher discontent) just skyrocketed. Mike was moved very quickly through the stages of Fisher's Process, from Happiness to Fear to Disillusionment, in less than a year's time.

In addition to the hardship created by Common Core curriculum, the Ohio State Standards testing was also judging the teens based on grade level, not developmental level, and it became abundantly clear that the charter school was expected to meet certain expectations. If they did not meet those expectations, there would be consequences for the charter school and its teachers.

"I liked my job, I enjoyed working with kids who have special needs, but I had been told at hiring that I would be a short-term hire." After the frustrating year of struggling uphill at his position, he also realized that no matter what public school he worked for, they would have those same Common Core curriculum standards and Ohio State Standards testing. Moving wasn't an option for Mike, his wife and their teenage children; and that wouldn't have fixed the issue anyhow, because all of the surrounding states had already instituted the Common Core curriculum. Mike found himself between a rock and hard place: keep working in a job whose performance standards seemed doomed to fail, or go back to his former profession as a surveyor and make more money: "the devil you know versus the devil you don't", he says.

Additionally, there were administration issues at the charter school. The school's lead administrator was a good person, but not in control of the Principal, who had terrible social and management skills, and had been observed verbally abusing both teachers and students. There was also the stress aspect of the population of students' demographics: 90% of the students were at or below poverty level, and had serious family issues that distracted or agitated them much of the time (including hunger, family violence, and living in dangerous neighborhoods). Mike had also had spent much time and energy in discussions with his wife, and in praying to God for guidance, before he had embarked on pursuing his teaching degree. "So, there is the 'what was the point of this' aspect of all of it." Mike felt that he had taken the decision seriously, but it still ended up in defeat.

And so, despite having gone back to university at the same time as his son, and graduating at the age of 45, Mike decided to cut his losses and return to his associate engineer position. Thankfully, he had continued doing that job on the weekends and knew his employer very well; otherwise, he may have had to start his employment search from scratch. The pay he had received as a teacher was paltry in comparison, but there was still disappointment over having failed at his attempt to re-route his career to something more suited to his desire to help people. Mike was also upset that his years in university, while working, had sometimes negatively affected his family life: "my schedule affected everybody. I had long days while in college, while also working; and then when I was teaching, I was up from five in the morning until midnight most days. To supplement my low teaching wage, I continued to do contracts on the side, and I also had paperwork that I took home every afternoon for my teaching job. We had just reached a breaking point."

There was also a significant relational cost to the decision to suspend his teaching career. "Some people in my life saw the decision as fruitless and foolhardy; but the money I made from contracts, and the overwhelming stress at my teaching job, made the decision for me." Because of the varying levels of support for whether Mike should have left teaching, he is still in the Depression stage of Fisher's Process, almost a year after the end of his teaching job. He is unsure of what the future holds, and how to grieve the loss of his dream of being a teacher.

Mike felt grateful that he could go immediately back to his associate engineering job. "I am respected by our customers, I have a good reputation, and existing customers have referred our company to new customers." He also felt an immediate relief of the stress that had been constantly pressing upon him during the school year. "I had started a new workout regimen that helped relieve stress, so that was good." Still, there is something missing: "When I was teaching, I was giving my students attention and showing them that someone loved them. I liked the idea that my job was self-sacrificial; that there was something important about what I did every day. 50% of the reason that I decided to quit teaching was the ridiculous testing standards; the other half of it was that I wasn't getting paid enough to take care of my family. If I had an option where I could have stayed in teaching and supported my family, I would have done that instead."

Mike has been discussing his long-term career options with his wife and doing online research. He has discovered that he can use his math education degree to work as an actuary, which is a position of risk prediction and management for all kinds of industries, including healthcare and insurance. It would entail setting aside time to study for the certification tests, which have five levels. Each level gains access to higher-paying positions with industries and corporations. Mike has already started reading the questions that have been included on previous tests, and thinks that he could be ready for the first level of certification tests in six months. "It seems like a promising lead, and if I left myself enough time to study, I wouldn't have to rush to take the first test, and it wouldn't have to take too much time away from my family."

Mike is considering the field of actuarial science because he has realized two things: that his wife feels very insecure about their financial future (he wants her to be content), and that they don't have enough money set aside for retirement. "Our present concerns are robbing us of a secure feeling for the future, and I don't want us to have financial anxiety."

Mike feels one comfort about this whole experience, which is that he made the decision to go back to school very convinced that it was God's will for him and his family. "So I have to believe that there was a higher (or future) purpose to it all, even though it was painful and disappointing."

Mike's advice to his children or other people of faith would be this: "God is not dumbfounded by your predicament, and he is not wringing his hands, nervously pacing back and forth wondering what to do next. It could very well be that failure is the only way to get you to where He needs you to be - either spiritually or literally. For example, if I am perfectly content living in Pennsylvania, but he wants me in Ohio, maybe a period of unemployment is precisely what is necessary to get me there. Here are a few things to do while waiting: First, do not dishonor God with your thoughts or words, calling into question His concern for you and your family. (Read the book of Job.) Second, commit your heart to purity in order to see God and to hear His voice. Third, find a way to delight in Him and commit to Him everything you do - and wait *patiently* for His provision. Fourth, don't waste time dwelling on the failures of the past. And finally, realize that it is God's job (and delight) to fulfill His purpose for you; let Him do it. (Psalm 138:8: The Lord will fulfill his purpose for me.)"

Nicole Steck: How Addiction Unravels A Family

Nicole Steck meets with me in a local restaurant edged with the sounds of businessmen on their lunch breaks, and televisions blaring baseball games and color commentary. Nicole is a pretty woman in her late 30's, with alert eyes and a sharp wit. When I describe the book project and its goals, she is very direct: "So do you want the abridged version of my story, or the full thing? Because it ain't pretty."

In November of 2003, Nicole thought things with her marriage were back on track. Her husband J. had admitted to his drinking problem, was regularly attending Alcoholic Anonymous meetings after work, and was cooperating with marriage counseling after a 4-month marital separation. It appeared that J. was also working on his marriage with Nicole. He was complying with certain requests to improve their marriage and his parenting of their two children, who were aged 3 years and 1 year at the time. And J.'s employers were friends with Nicole, knew that the couple was in counseling for their marriage and that J. was trying to straighten out his life.

Suddenly, Nicole received a phone call that changed her family's life forever. "A friend from J.'s work called and told me everything that had been going on behind the scenes: J. had been going to bars instead of AA meetings, was drinking constantly and asking coworkers for a big personal loan in the thousands of dollars. J. had been making bets on the side, and had bookies showing up to work looking for him." He had also taken money from his 401K to pay some of his gambling debts. J. had been fired that day, and this work friend wanted Nicole to know EXACTLY what J. had been up to, "so that I could make decisions based on real information and not the fantasy that J. had been trying to sell me for months." The caller was very sympathetic about Nicole's situation and wanted her to have the whole truth.

Nicole had to think fast; "if J. had a gambling problem, that combined with the drinking problem would mean that the remainder of our assets were at risk, and financial provision for my children was on the line." She had a lot of work to do to protect her family, and not a lot of time to do it. And she could read the writing on the wall: if J. had invested that much time and energy in (again) misleading her, their marriage was pretty much over. The broken trust would never be recovered.

"I called my parents and revealed to them what had happened that day." They encouraged her to again separate from J. to protect the children and the family assets. She consulted a family member who was an attorney, and arranged for their bank accounts to be "frozen" so that J. could not gamble away their remaining money.

That night when J. came home, Nicole told him that he was no longer welcome in their house, and that he had better find a rehabilitation program and immediately register himself in said program. Nicole packed overnight bags for her and the children, and immediately went to her parents' house. They stayed there for a couple of days, until J. left for rehab.

"I went back to the house and tried to find a new 'normal' for the kids. I called an old work buddy from five years back, from a job I had been at when J. and I met. He was now at a new company, and arranged for my resume to bypass the usual route and gave it straight to the Vice President of the company. He vouched for me and asked for a fair salary, one on which I could support my family. I quickly interviewed for that position and was hired. They agreed to suspend the position for four weeks so that I could get everything arranged for the divorce."

Nicole found herself in the middle of the dissolution of the marriage and being enlightened as to J.'s long-term financial cover up. About a week after she had gone back to the house with the kids, she received a box of belongings from J's old job. It was full of old, unpaid bills and collection notices. "It painted a horrible picture: of the web of lies J. had created, and the lengths he had gone to in order to cover up his drinking and his gambling. I went into survival mode, calling utility companies and realizing that they had shut down his accounts for nonpayment. I went in person to set up all the utilities in my own name, which was so surreal. It was very symbolic of the solitary path I was about to take, as a single mom and divorced woman."

For three years, Nicole had been a stay at home mom. She had been able to attend to her children's needs full time, and give them the attention that they needed. Now she found herself divided between their care and the arrangements needed for their new life: "It was pretty much a fulltime job for a few weeks, making phone calls, negotiating with companies we owed money to, communicating with the attorney and my new employer. My new employer agreed to bypass the standard three-month temp status for my position, which meant that I had immediate benefits coverage for our family. I was also busy scrambling to find a new home for us, something more within our new budget. I quickly found an apartment that we could afford on my new salary. We had to foreclose on our home, because J. refused to sign a listing agreement for a proper sale of our home. He was that spiteful about our marriage dissolving right in front of him."

J. had completed the two weeks of the rehab program, but resisted the idea of divorce even though Nicole filed at the end of November 2003. Nicole worked closely with the attorney to negotiate child support arrangements, her parents helped to take care of the kids, and Nicole started her new job in December of that year. "I saw a network of support fall into place as family, close friends and members of my Christian community responded to our situation. My friend Joe gave me a car to use while he was deployed in Iraq. The apartment that was offered to us was in the same town where our house was, and was close to my new job and friends who were very supportive of us. There are two friends in our Christian group who experienced divorce and had good wisdom to offer me; and one relative who had gone through it.

Their stories gave me perspective on my situation and made me grateful over time. I also went to counseling with the therapist who had done our marriage counseling." Nicole also received practical help, such as grocery store gift cards and money to help her cover Catholic marriage annulment costs (at the end of 2004, a year after the divorce was completed); and spiritual support from Koinonia, a local young adults' Christian group and its members. "And my parents were so supportive without being suffocating, there was no judgment for how my marriage ended, and they were a safe support."

Nicole was helping her children adjust to the divorce, and it was very difficult on the first day that she had to take them to daycare to start her new job. "Here I am, dropping them off to strangers after the breakup, feeling uncomfortable and guilty about having to go back to work, and I had to look strong and BE strong for my children. J. had put me in the position of making these changes, these decisions, and filing for divorce, and it made me very sad and upset." Nicole was in the Anxiety Phase of Fisher's Process of Transition: trying to work around events that are being orchestrated outside of one's control, adjusting to a new work environment, unsure as to what the new rules are for operating within the work environment.

"Our new normal was us three going everywhere together: church, grocery shopping, visits with friends. I felt the full weight of being a single mom, and it was difficult to find a work/life balance. I did get in a regular exercise routine, which worked as a combination of distraction and self-care (and it was the one thing that I could control at the time; I was responsible for self-discipline and self-control, no one else)." Nicole had a daily routine with the kids, and having a sense of humor helped too. Additionally, she reconnected with friends and socialized in a way that she hadn't been able to do when her family life had previously been so unpredictable.

During Nicole's adjustment to re-entering the workforce, she noticed that her new office was a sort of "meat market atmosphere; on the one hand, it was uncomfortable, on the other: somewhat empowering. The attention sort of bolstered my womanly confidence." Nicole missed spending a lot of time with her kids, and setting her own schedule as a stay at home mom; but she really enjoyed getting to have conversations with other adults, the mental stimulation and external validation of a challenging job. Nicole had moved into the Gradual Acceptance phase of Fisher's Process. She was starting to gain more control over managing the work and home changes, which has links to a higher level of self-confidence and self-mastery.

For 18 months, Nicole and her children lived in the apartment down the road from their foreclosed home, which allowed them to see their friends and socialize on the weekends. Nicole was then able to then find an apartment next to her parents' home, in her own hometown, "which felt like coming home again, and felt so positive and permanent." Nicole's Christian faith really sustained her during this time, as did her parents' love and support, and her friends in Koinonia. She also eventually dated and remarried, and has regained her stay at home parent role, an intact family structure, and familial stability.

Nicole's advice to others: "Think really, really hard before you marry someone. It is harder to divorce a narcissist than to marry one. You should probably date someone a year (or more) before you get married; that gives you time to see what their background and flaws are, how they react to stress. Don't just fall into a relationship or marriage; pray before every step, and have others pray with you. Try to figure out, what is God's will for my life, and for this process?"

Traumatic vocational transitions can happen because of the actions of an employer, as when an employee is forcibly retired, laid off, fired, or demoted:

Dr. John Clarke: Grace Under Fire*

Dr. John Clarke and I meet in the light-filled sunroom of his family's home in suburban Pittsburgh. The narrow, steep steps to the second floor stand out as an architectural signature of older Pittsburgh homes, as does the small living room with fireplace and large dining room adjacent to the kitchen. Dr. Clarke is a quiet, intelligent man who takes time to mull over each question to ensure that he responds honestly and completely, and I appreciate the consideration and seriousness with which he approaches the interviewing process.

Dr. John Clarke is an Associate Professor at a Christian university in the Midwest. At age 62, Dr. Clarke has an impressive resume, including two Masters Degrees and a Doctorate in Clinical Psychology. He also has a part-time position as a Senior Mental Health Consultant for a vocational training program in a nearby city. Dr. Clarke's most recent vocational transition was sudden and complex. "In a short span of time, my department's work space was abruptly moved to a different part of campus and downsized; our class space was lost; and most impactful was my removal as Chair of the department." His co-workers, including several full-time faculty, a secretary, and five or six adjuncts were surprised by the changes, and both the department team and their student body were affected by these decisions. The decision that was foisted on Dr. Clarke pushed him into the Depression and Hostility Phases of Fisher's Transition Process.

Dr. Clarke feels that "the decisions were abrupt, and communication regarding these issues was obscure and at times, puzzling. Our department was pursuing professional accreditation, and the whole team was concentrating on completing the proposal for the accrediting body, especially since we were under a time constraint. We wanted to ensure that students who were getting ready to graduate would have the accreditation attached to their graduation credits. We wanted to do our due diligence to make sure that the graduates would have that as an educational and professional benefit."

Dr. Clarke's removal as Chair of his department was unexpected and had a negative effect (at least temporarily) on his view of the university. The human fallibility of the people involved in that decision (and their communication flaws) had a startling, bracing effect on the Dr.'s perception of how a Christian university (and its leaders) should behave. "The main explanation that was given was that the department policy regarding how long a person should be Chair had been changed, and that seven years was "enough time" for one person." That the communication provided ahead of time was murky, and that the decision was finalized without explanation or apology for its abruptness, furthered the personal hurt experienced by Dr. Clarke during his transition out of that position. "I felt that my decision to speak up about how our department had been moved; our office space downsized; and our designated classroom space eliminated, probably contributed to the decision to remove me as Chair." Dr. Clarke had stood up for his department when he felt that the needs of his department and its students were not being met, and that their voices weren't being heard by the administrators. His career was seriously affected by that stance. It was the most significant political experience of his university career.

"A majority of the support during this difficult time came from my wife of 35+ years" who helped him by coming alongside him and spending time with him, including their shared pastime of bicycling. Dr. Clarke also has Christian friends who prayed with him, and helped him to recognize that his worth doesn't come from his career, and that accepting the turn that his life was taking would help him to stay positive and clear-headed. "Additionally, I have two other friends who are professors at the same university that I have bonded with through teamwork and the accreditation proposal, and now we have a shared experience that made the bond even stronger."

Time with family, friends, and fellow Christians created additional supports that helped Dr. Clarke to keep things in perspective, and to find the good in a difficult situation. "I have come to realize that the relief that I have experienced by leaving the Chair position behind has lessened my overall stress." He doesn't miss the politics involved in that position, nor the administrative work involved, including evaluations for two of his fellow professors in the department.

Now that Dr. Clarke has had some time to step back, look at the situation, and assess the pros and cons of the results of these decisions, he has discovered some things about himself (and the university). "I have come to realize that I was putting more of my personal identity in my career than I previously thought." He now also understands that he assumed that some of the decisions that were made were personal, when they were probably professional decisions that would have been made regardless of the surrounding circumstances. "I also see now that some 'olive branches' were extended by the administrators, such as shared teamwork and committee work". Dr. Clarke's reflection on the previous year of his career have brought him first to the Gradual Acceptance and then to the Moving Forward stage of Fisher's Model; he can see himself in the "new" future, and what his part is in that future.

Dr. Clarke's advice on vocational transitions is this: "Don't take things too personally; add time to how long you think the transitions will take; and don't establish your overall life purpose in your career." He feels that he will benefit from the time that has been freed up because of this experience, and he is looking forward to new opportunities and experiences with university students that the additional class time will provide.

Mae Legaspi: A Hit Out of Left Field

Mae Legaspi and I meet on my back porch on a sticky August afternoon in 2015. The sky alternates between sunny skies and grey storm clouds as we talk, between still air and breezy surprises. Mae is from the Philippines, and traveled to Pittsburgh for an international meeting of professional women who are "single for the Lord" called The Bethany Association, a group of Christian women who discern that their lives are meant to be lived set apart for a special purpose to serve God and his people. This status vocation is most times permanent; but I have heard of those who have been called out of single life because of providential meetings with future spouses, or because of discernment that they were mistaken about that vocation in the first place (ie: Frank Stuparitz, mentioned earlier in this chapter).

"Us women in international Christian communities who choose singleness as a vocation have a small but vigorous group of supporters who pray for us, keep up communication (even across the globe), and share challenges, victories and goals with each other," Mae says, "it is a sort of sisterhood unlike any other I have seen." This writer is personally acquainted with a Pittsburgh member of The Bethany Association who has shared with others her decision to become single for the Lord, and answered many awkward questions regarding that decision. Mae Legaspi is one of many women across the world who have chosen singlehood in a purposeful manner, not out of default from not finding a spouse. "But I am here to share with you another journey, one I didn't willingly begin, but one that has taught me many things about inner strength and choices." It is also a story about transforming adversity into opportunity.

Mae Legaspi is 66 years old and well-educated. She earned her bachelor's degree in teaching from the Philippine Normal University in Manila, Philippines in 1968. In 1997 she achieved her master's degree in Family Dynamics & Ministry from Ateneo de Manila University, the third oldest university in the Philippines and a Jesuit university that has been in existence since 1859. At the same time, Mae was working full time for her ecumenical (includes all Christian denominations) Christian community called Ligaya ng Panginoon, meaning Joy of the Lord, which belongs to the Sword of the Spirit International (an association of ecumenical communities worldwide). Mae's areas of responsibility included pastoral work, counseling (life coach), evangelization of new members, and community building. Mae had been working for the community for 20 years, and was looking forward to using her newly-earned master's to enhance her work with community members and for evangelization purposes. "I love our community, we have many things to offer that local churches cannot do, especially in the areas of youth work and personal spiritual development."

In 1997, Mae was abruptly informed that her full time paid position of community work was being eliminated because the community leaders had decided to remove paid pastoral workers from the budget. "It was like someone had pulled the floor out from under me! It took me right back to 1990, when the development of our local Filipino sisterhood chapter was abruptly halted, because the hosting community in the United States had fractured, and our sisterhood had no one to supervise it. We three sisters in the Filipino community were suddenly adrift, with no supervision or direction! The international association of Bethany didn't exist yet, and so we felt completely disoriented." Mae again experienced that disorientation in 1997 as she practically panicked; she had an elderly mother to take care of, a home to maintain and bills to pay. As a single person, she was wholly financially responsible for herself, and had no one to fall back on. The possible effects of unemployment on unmarried workers is vast, including declining health (because of loss of health insurance), elevated levels of mental health problems (due to the uncertainty of financial and other provisions), and an increase in family stress due to uncertainty of finances.

Temporarily, Mae's community leaders agreed to help financially support Mae until she found adequate employment, but her adjustment to unemployed life was still difficult. "I had poured all my life, energy and joy into my work, was still really productive and effective, and suddenly it was gone. I still helped our community with pastoral work in small groups and such, but that full-time energetic work life was gone. I was asking questions of myself like 'Who am I?' and 'What am I supposed to do with my life?' I knew the answer was NOT to leave our community to seek a pastoral work position elsewhere; all of my friends and family and community friends are here in Quezon City. And in 1996, when my dad died, I had become the matriarch of our family and had carried many responsibilities that went along with being matriarch." Filipino society is matriarchal in nature, and most women hold positions of esteem and power in their families, and hold financial roles equal to their husbands or brothers (source: Global Affairs Canada, 2017).

When Filipino parents are elderly and one parent dies, the eldest sibling typically takes the responsibility of mediating decisions for the family, which is how Mae became the matriarch. In a short span of time, Mae experienced the Fear, Anger, Guilt and Depression Stages of Fisher's Process. To move into the Gradual Acceptance Stage, Mae had to share her uncertain, negative and ambiguous feelings with her support system, including her small group in community and her pastoral worker (a combination of friend and spiritual advisor that community members willingly accept as part of community life). She processed through her disappointment, anger, embarrassment, confusion, and fear. "I prayed a lot, talked to God, used my journal and retreats to get through it. I talked to my other friends in the sisterhood and figured out what to do next." Another therapeutic type of self-care that Mae engaged in was walking. She found that being in nature helped her to breathe a little, have a respite from her responsibilities at home, and she enjoyed looking at God's creation while walking.

Mae received extensive support for this transition, but she does have some regrets about how she handled the situation. "I wish that I had talked to someone about how to "face" this unwanted change, to help me to better accept it and to move forward faster, instead of staying in the grief." Mae also felt some anger towards someone whom she relied on for support, but who was so distracted by her own painful personal situation that she was not able to be supportive for Mae. She did, however, receive extensive personal support from another friend in the sisterhood, and a male friend who is also "single for the Lord".

In 2000, a fellow member of her Christian community invited her to interview with a local consulting company. He mentored Mae before and after the interview, and was also her trainer for her consulting position. The position involved management consulting in the area of organizational development, which utilized both her undergraduate and graduate degrees. The company provides services for corporations and nonprofit companies. It was a good paid position, but was very fast-paced, and Mae had to stop volunteering for community because she had no 'extra' time.

The new position was challenging, and very different from her previous career. In her pastoral and evangelism roles in community, Mae had been responsible for the spiritual development of other people, and felt that she had an eternal impact on people's lives, especially by evangelizing. In this new role, she was responsible for communication and consultation with multinational corporations, which expanded her worldview. It was fast-paced and a considerable intellectual challenge as well, because each client and their needs were different from the one before. "I was constantly required to think outside of the box, to use all of my intellectual and creative gifts, and it was rewarding, to see that I could do something new and succeed at it."

There were two difficult things about this new position, however: "The commute was very tiring, and we had to make quota. I wasn't used to that!" She also felt that the corporate atmosphere didn't really suit her preference for a personal touch and direct work with individual people.

Eventually, Mae reached the Disillusionment Phase, and decided to leave the firm in 2005 to open her own small consulting firm. "My experience at the firm gave me the experience, training, and confidence to develop my own company and establish my own clientele." Opening her own firm helped to satisfy her preference for having more direct contact with individuals in companies, and for being in control of projects. It also allowed her to work from home and attend to her mother, who shared a home with Mae. Unfortunately, Mae's mother's health continued to decline, and by 2010 she required Mae's 24-hour supervision and care. Mae closed her firm that year to care for her mother, who became weaker, soon lost muscle memory and was only able to process liquified foods.

For four years, Mae cared for her mother at home and full-time. Her decisions were shaped by her mom's needs first, and she tried to steal little moments of time for self-care, like walking or getting manicures. On August 23, 2014, Mae's mother temporarily stopped breathing as Mae was shifting her body around while changing linens. She died the next day. "It was an honor to care for my mother, especially in her last year. I preferred to care for her, instead of a stranger, even instead of a friend. I was able to be by her side as she passed away. That was a privilege!"

Mae is in the Gradual Acceptance phase of Fisher's Process, both in her adjustment to her life without her mother, and in her new role as a high school student life coach (helping with college preparation, etc.). Additionally, she is being trained to extend her work beyond the university-aged group of young adults. At some point, she may consider restarting her small business. "I am still energetic and active, and believe that I have much to offer as a mentor and guide to younger generations."

Mae also has continued volunteer work for her Christian community as a senior women's leader. She trains younger women into leadership in the community, and travels within the Philippines and other parts of Asia to help develop newer Christian communities that belong to the Sword of the Spirit ecumenical association of communities. "It is an exciting aspect of my work within community, that I get to work with new communities and to watch them grow!"

Mae's advice to other people facing sudden job loss? "You need help to see through your own emotions, someone more neutral. Discuss the matter with someone you trust and can be yourself with, but who is capable and objective, someone who can help to prevent you from getting stuck. Do everything you can to not get stuck in the grief, as you can become directionless, and find yourself living in the past. Set aside your fear of change! Have an open mind, and identify your transferable skills. Also, can you go outside of yourself and volunteer or minister to others? That would be a good distraction. Try to see beyond this, down the road: what are the advantages of the process you are going through? And how can you move on?"

Moving on is a common theme in vocational transition stories; for some, moving on means changing career paths to experience personal or intellectual rejuvenation. For others, moving on is a means of psychological or practical survival because of the abandonment of a spouse or partner:

Teresa McLaughlin: Paying the Price for Arrested Development

During the fall of 2015 Teresa McLaughlin nervously settles in at my dining room table, not sure what to expect. She pushes her dark hair behind one ear and looks out the window when describing the painful parts of her story. I offer her a pseudonym to make the process easier, but Teresa is insistent that she be open and honest about the complicated nature of her experience as a single mom and provider for her children, and that includes her identity.

Full disclosure: I have known Teresa McLaughlin my whole life, and so am inclined to believe her "version" of the story. She doesn't hide her own faults, is merciful to others, and is delicately honest regarding her divorce and the resulting familial and functional effects. Also, I am kind of partial to her; she is my sister. But also, there is this: single mothers (functionally, psychologically and often economically) have the lion's share of responsibility after divorce, and handle the aftereffects with the children much more than fathers do (Kramer, 2015).

Having personally watched several family members go through the process of separation, divorce, reconfiguration of family dynamics, and then remarriage, several themes stand out in bas relief against the backdrop of this family experience:

1) Loss and grief;
2) Personal strength and weakness;
3) And reimagining the future: relationally, economically, functionally and vocationally.

Realistically, about half of all American marriages will end in divorce. This accounts for the prevalence of multiple divorces in a lifetime for some people (Banschick, 2012), and is reflected in the negative results of divorce on women's economic security (Landers, 2011) and on children's economic well-being (Reilly, 2009).

Teresa McLaughlin never imagined that she would be a single mother, which is a familiar story. "Women marry and imagine raising their children with their spouses, growing old together, and finishing their stories in the house in which their children grew up. But on August 17, 2009, after a long pattern of shady behavior, immaturity, and suspicions of current infidelity, I confronted my husband about an affair that he had been having." Her spouse, S., admitted to the affair over the phone and then they argued in person. This affair had come after 17 years as a couple (12 of them married), and a long history of S. making rash and immature decisions regarding his social life and their family life. Teresa, on the other hand, had consistently worked to establish an equitable marriage. She believed in working to help support their family, and had worked in either nursing or home-based childcare their whole marriage. At the time of S.'s affair, Teresa provided childcare in her home for a friend's grandchild and was a stay at home mother for their three children. Because S. insisted that he was in love with both Teresa and his girlfriend, Teresa then insisted that he make a choice (both for her sanity and for her dignity). S. could not make the choice, so Teresa made it for him, and filed for divorce in October of 2009. Teresa filed online for a no-contest divorce, paid the $450 fee, and then calculated online what would be fair for child support and gave that information to S. Teresa's husband agreed to all her terms.

After that, subsequent decisions happened very quickly. Teresa and S. could not afford to keep their large house AND an apartment for S., so their family home went on the market in November of 2009. In the same month, Teresa decided to go back into nursing and applied for a second job in home health. "I felt a lot of internal pressure to get another job, and I also quickly realized that keeping busy and providing for my children helped to keep me distracted from the failure of my marriage."

At the same time Teresa was mourning the demise of her marriage and the dissolution of their family, vocationally she was experiencing the Fear and Threat Phases of Fisher's Process: "I knew that I needed to get back out there and make more money than I could make in childcare, and I felt that it was my job now to find money in different places: by selling our house and getting another job, whatever I could do. I felt an urgency and a push to keep DOING." In October of 2009, Teresa contacted the renters of her previous family home and informed them that she would have to move back in there with the kids (they were very gracious). In November, she started her new job as a home health nurse. Her youngest son had started kindergarten that fall, so she just had to work around the schedule of the child she provided childcare for.

"I also had to make time to attend to the needs of our three children, who were all adjusting to the 'new normal' of our divorce and the visitation schedule; staging our large family home to get it ready for the housing market, which was terrible at the time; and trying to take time for myself to absorb and pay attention to what was happening to my life. I was losing not just S., but his family too. We had been dating since I was 14 years old, and when the divorce happened (even though it was S.'s fault), his family felt a loyalty and started to separate themselves from my life. I had been good friends with S.'s mother and aunt, they were a huge emotional support during our marriage, and now they were distant."

The other griefs were more consistent and predictable: letting go of their large beautiful home, which sold in January of 2010, was a symbolic move and very hurtful. "We had been doing so well, had moved out of our other house which had become too small for us, and here we are: moving back in and now without S." There was also the embarrassment and guilt over S.'s affair and the subsequent divorce (because when you raise your family in a small town, nothing goes unnoticed), though the largest source of personal grief that Teresa experienced was having to come to terms with her part in how the marriage fell apart. "I realized that all of the ways that S.'s mother had catered to him and coddled him, I had continued that as a wife. I indulged his temper tantrums and tried to soothe him. I didn't insist on total transparency about how he spent his personal time, and with whom he spent it. I allowed S. to stay dominant in our family life, and inadvertently allowed him to be infantile. We had been together for so long that I just kept doing what I knew would keep him happy, and he just never grew up." Especially when it came to S.'s personal privacy, Teresa had good boundaries, but that allowed S. to carry on in an affair almost totally undetected: "The times that I checked his phone and found anything suspicious was early on in the affair, and they were personal texts but not intimate. He insisted that they were just friends, that because she was a new employee at the car dealership, he was just being friendly. Later I found out that they had stopped texting altogether, and just left voicemail messages for each other in their cell phones, which are gone once you erase them." Though there were red flags, none of them were glaring enough to catch her eye: "He started saying things about being grateful for me, that I didn't have to take care of him so much, etc. I should have been suspicious, because he had always taken that for granted, that it was just part of my job as a wife."

    As far as Teresa's work life was concerned, it had fallen into a predictable pattern of home health care work and providing childcare. "I did feel resentful; I wasn't the one who messed up, but had to go back to work full-time and also make sure my kids were okay with all of these huge changes. I was tired a lot, but also needed the distraction of being 'too busy', you know? And I was getting a lot of advice from a lot of people, from all of those who loved me and meant well, but it was just - exhausting." Teresa was experiencing the Depression and Hostility Phases ("I'll make this work if it kills me!") of Fisher's Process.

    When Teresa and S.'s house sold in January of 2010 (the same month that the divorce went through), Teresa felt a load lifted from her. "Although we sold it for the same amount we had bought it for, it was one more burden and debt off of my mind. I was sad we had to sell it, but relieved when it did. Especially since it was the last aspect of shared financial connection between me and S." The reactions of Teresa's children were mixed; at least one of her children was happy to move back into the smaller house where so many happy family memories had been made, but one of them was not happy with the change of scenery. Teresa had to soothe that child, and explain that it was a necessary part of their family transition. "They also had kind of chaotic schedules, now that I look back; they were with our sister Chrissy a lot, after school and during the summers while I worked. I also enlisted my (ex)mother-in-law for help with the kids. We were going through family counseling, to help me and my kids adjust to the divorce and find our 'new normal'. I was meeting with an annulment representative in our Catholic diocese, to pursue a religious annulment because of S's affair, so that I could choose to marry in the church again in the future. **And** I was going through how to define myself as a single mom: what did it mean to me?"

Teresa's whole life felt chaotic during this time; her jobs, her responsibilities, negotiating aspects of co-parenting with her ex, establishing boundaries with him and his family: "I was doing all of it in a fog. I started Divorce Care and also Fresh Start; they both helped me to see that when my ex talked about missing our life together, he always centered on missing us as a family, missing our kids, missing our old house. But he never used language that he actually missed ME. Support groups helped me to see what his intentions and motivations were, and made me even more resolved to have good boundaries with him."

When asked what she did with all the uncomfortable feelings around this time, Teresa laughs: "I DANCED! I went out with my nieces and friends and danced off the stress. I also prayed so much more; I felt so close to God during that time. I pleaded with God to help me to get through all of it."

And, "Not everything that came from being divorced was bad. My divorce helped to humble me, to grow my empathy for others, and in compassion too. My job, also, helped me to do that; home health care put me right into people's homes and lives, into the middle of it. It took me to the poverty areas of Pittsburgh and right into my clients' homes. I wouldn't have had those experiences if I hadn't decided to do that job."

But these are the things that she lost because of the divorce, when she lost her ability to be a stay at home mom: "I wasn't always available to be with my sick or hurt kids, so it would be other people taking care of them when that happened, my sister or S.'s mom. I missed feeling 'caught up' in my home life responsibilities, home repairs had to wait, home improvements had to wait, I had very long days because of work and doing everything at home by myself. I also have to carefully plan my time with sisters or friends, I can't just be spontaneous, my availability for others is carefully planned."

What doesn't she miss about being a stay at home mom? "Because my kids were so little and close in age, I never got any rest! And also, I don't miss the disrespect you get from others when you tell them you are a stay at home mom. No matter how busy I was, there were intrusive questions about what I was going to do when the kids were in school full time, or about not being busy because I was a stay at home mom. That was crazy! Because I was always so busy."

Teresa's top three supports during this time were God (via prayer, during which she learned to see herself through God's eyes), the support and advice of family and friends, and defining her identity as a child of God first (and not through anyone else's world view). Also, "the marriage annulment process helped me to examine how my marriage had fallen apart, to own any of my responsibility for that, and to let go of the rest."

Teresa remarried in 2014, and now works as a nurse in cardiac testing labs. With three teenagers and three stepchildren, she has no plan to change jobs: "No, I make too much money to consider a change! We have a big family and a big house, and we will both keep working no matter what." Teresa is seated firmly in the Moving Forward stage of Fisher's Process, is content in her job and in her life and has no plans to make any changes.

Teresa's advice to other moms faced with a similar situation? "Find something flexible and part-time so that your kids can have you as much as possible. Don't prioritize being busy over spending time with your kids, or taking care of yourself; it's not healthy and your relationships will suffer because of it. Lastly: experience life! Do things that you love and have fun with your friends before you decide to start dating again. Take care of your SELF before you decide to marry again."

Chapter 7:
Fresh Starts: How to Think Outside of the Box

One of the most intimidating pursuits that an adult may experience is the decision to voluntarily change career paths. There are lots of reasons why this may be true:
- A high-paying job is hard to find in some geographical areas.
- Social pressure: "Don't look a gift horse in the mouth!"
- A spouse or significant other may not support the decision to leave a stable job to take a risk in a completely different career field.
- The pressure of providing for a family can be a real and significant responsibility, so you decide to "let sleeping dogs lie."

- You are interested in a new, niche field that carries significant risk, either financially or professionally.
- You are interested in starting your own small business, which can have the added burden of providing health insurance, retirement or other benefits for someone other than yourself.
- You are in your 50's or 60's, and potential professional failure carries with it the risk of wrecking your retirement finances.
- And lastly: going out of our comfort zone is something most humans tend to avoid, whenever possible: "Why rock the boat??"

There are, however, very significant scenarios in which a total career change is necessary: (Caprino, 2013)
- You are chronically worn out, exhausted and depleted.
- Your responsibilities, tasks and skills are not "you", at all.
- Your salary no longer makes up for the boredom and emptiness that you feel.
- Despite having followed all the "right steps", the outcome feels very wrong.
- You have the feeling that your talents, abilities and gifts should/could be used in a totally different way.

The perfect example of a necessary career change can be best illustrated through the story of Lulu Orr:

Lulu Orr: Why *Not* Reinvent Yourself?

Parking at a downtown Pittsburgh underground lot, I make my way up urine-scented stairways and through heavy metal doors to enter blinding sunlight bouncing off skyscrapers, cars, and department store windows. Walking several blocks of city sidewalks can be time-consuming and tricky: I navigate around small groups of women in business suits, chatting and gesticulating with lit cigarettes. I also dodge rickety metal doors in the sidewalk, newspaper blowing up from the gutters, and try to find the address while squinting in the sunshine (I have been spoiled by suburban living).

I arrive at my destination, and enter a luxuriously appointed lobby whose shiny atmosphere is somewhat marred by a utilitarian security checkpoint. I procure a magnetic pass after providing a driver's license, and take the elevator seven floors skyward while humming along to Enya being piped through an invisible speaker. I arrive to a quiet selection of suites and am greeted by a soft-spoken and well-dressed secretary. (By now, I am nervous: will I be taken seriously? Am I dressed too sloppy for a downtown interview? WHAT AM I DOING HERE? Of course, this being my very first interview for my book, such nonsense is understandable.)

Lulu Orr quickly dispels my nervousness, grasping my hand in a firm and friendly handshake, offering me coffee (liquid courage, I like to call it), and guiding me to a conference room which is more "university" and less high-powered than I expected. Lulu's relaxed, professional and down-to-earth demeanor immediately disarms me. She asks a lot of questions about the goal of the book, and on the topic of vocational transitions and vocational grieving, and then we begin.

Lulu, age 55, is the founder of Good Grief, a nonprofit agency in Pittsburgh, Pennsylvania which provides support and counseling throughout the grieving process. "In 2010, after almost ten years of leading the agency, I felt that my time with the center should come to an end, and that I should transition the existing partners and board to run the agency without me."

"Together with advice from my husband, I decided to take a year off from work to discover myself. I had spent so many years at Good Grief developing the identity of the agency, raising money (and being the face of the agency), that I had kind of lost sight of who I was, separate from the agency." Lulu had arrived at the Disillusionment stage of Fisher's Process.

Lulu had professional and personal confidence that the existing Associate Director could be trusted with the agency, and so handing over the reins was a natural process. "I also ensured that the agency leadership team had almost a full year with me before I resigned." Lulu made a total mental break from the agency, and did not continue as a consultant or advisor; she was in the next to last step of Fisher's Process of Transition, Gradual Acceptance.

During her year off, Lulu spent much of her time in various personal pursuits, and spent time with family and friends. She had conversations with her (deceased) father, asking for guidance in exploring options for herself. "My husband and children were also key 'life support' during that time; family was totally honest with me during that time, and I value their advice." At the beginning of this vocational transition, she also spent a lot of time in phone conversations with her three sisters as they walked together through emotionally processing the physical deterioration of their mother, and then their mother's death.

What did Lulu miss the most about her work at the agency? "The people! The team had a shared mission, vision and purpose." They had common work bonds, but also compatible personalities.

"What I don't miss is the constant struggle to find money with which to run the agency." There was considerable time spent trying to convince others of the agency's purpose and usefulness, perhaps because the urban atmosphere of Pittsburgh meant that she was competing with many other nonprofit agencies for the same pool of donor funds.

After her year off, Lulu entered the last step of the Process of Transition, Moving Forward. She found part-time employment with a company that provides guidance for the governance boards of nonprofit companies in the Pittsburgh area. She leaves work at work, and her identity lies squarely in her own hands as she grows in her relationship with her husband and grown children; her identity is her whole self and not in the work functions she performs every day. Her advice to those going through similar metamorphosis? "Do what you love. Take the time to figure that out. Find out what makes you happy and not just what makes you money. Find what brings meaning and passion to your life!"

Paul Abernathy: Syria, Suffering, and Service

Paul Abernathy meets me at an urban location in the Hill District of Pittsburgh, the office of his current vocation, FOCUS Pittsburgh. The setting is a storefront, with the service area of the charity on the first floor, boxes of sorted clothing donations on one side, tables with sorted food donations on the other. Orthodox icons of saints and other religious art adorn one wall, old and comfortable furniture in a seating array on the opposite side. Paul leads me out the front door, to another door to the left of the storefront, and we walk up a narrow, ancient wooden staircase to the second floor. His wife introduces herself and welcomes me to the center, and then quietly exits, as Paul relaxes into his office chair. His eyes light up as he takes me on a linguistic, global tour of his complex vocational path:

One of the pivotal experiences in Paul Abernathy's life was on a visit to Damascus, Syria (his mother's homeland) in 2005. "During that trip I saw firsthand the political, religious, and cultural tension that was coming to a head in the region, and I was deeply concerned." He observed the region's Christian population coming to terms with their possible martyrdom for the faith, as more restrictions, laws and constrictions were put in place to control their rights and actions. "I knew enough about the history of the region to know that these trends were a precursor to full persecution of my Christian friends and relatives in Syria." The statistics (*as of 2015) have brought to bear that belief as fact: less than 400,000 Christians are still living in Syria, down from 1.1 million in 2010; a drastic reduction from the 1.7 million Christians who lived in Syria in 2003 (Di Giovanni & Gaffey, 2015). The Christian Syrians are fleeing to avoid persecution, physical abuse, retaliation from ISIS soldiers, beheadings, forced conversion to Islam, and other war crimes such as rape.

Paul returned from Syria with a renewed vigor for his Christian faith, and with the idea to consider martyrdom of his own comfort in the service of God's people. "My grandmother and mother, who are devout Catholics, raised me and my sister in an atmosphere of humble simplicity. They raised me with a spiritual foundation that I depend upon." Paul's mother was a social worker and worked in hospice care, and understands working in service of others. She has been very supportive of him over the years as he followed his path from high school to higher education at Wheeling Jesuit University in International Studies. Paul's family had also been a major core of support as he served in the United States Army as an enlisted and then Reserves soldier, which eventually led to his participation in the very first day of the ground war in Iraq on March 19, 2003. When Paul returned from active duty, he decided to return to college to achieve a graduate degree. Paul earned a master's degree in Public & International Affairs at the University of Pittsburgh, and during this time experienced the Disillusionment stage of Fisher's Process.

"I knew that I would not be happy with pursuing a business career", and he had sensed that he was reaching a spiritually-significant shift in his career goals: to choose between a life of earning potential and careerism and one of lifelong service in religious vocations. Paul grasped the connection between being a Christian and living a life of service. He knew that a call to seminary would mean a life of vocation and sacrifice, and that the corporate life was not for him.

After his masters from the University of Pittsburgh was completed, he felt the draw towards seminary and applied. He was initially reluctant because St. Tikhon's Seminary in rural Pennsylvania was geographically isolated, but also because he had started getting lucrative job offers. "I knew that I had to make a choice between two good futures."

Paul saw that he was leaving behind a "professional life," and many of the Orthodox priests in seminary nurtured him away from seeing that as a negative aspect of being ordained. Paul achieved his masters of Divinity from St. Tikhon's Orthodox Theological Seminary in 2010. This degree eventually led to his ordination as an Orthodox priest in the fall of 2016.

Paul is incredibly grateful and effusive regarding the many people who guided, mentored, and advised him during critical junctures of his vocational and faith journeys. "I credit growth in my personal diplomacy to Father Dan Joyce", a priest who displayed much kindness to Paul and other Wheeling Jesuit students who participated in the Mother Jones House, an intentional Christian service community in Wheeling, West Virginia. While participating in Mother Jones, students receive greatly reduced room and board in exchange for ten hours of service a week to the surrounding community. They also receive an AmeriCorps Education Award of $1,000 at the end of the year. The six core values of Mother Jones House are simplicity, faith, community, social justice, learning and service. The House's stated motto is "Pray for the dead, and fight like hell for the living".

During his time at Mother Jones House, Paul also worked as a Coordinator for Community Research and Project Development. During that experience, Father Dan Joyce mentored Paul as he negotiated through difficult situations that arose from meetings with local community leaders. Father Dan sent Paul to these meetings alone, and then would reflect with Paul to help him discover what motivated these leaders, and how to utilize that information to connect with them to develop cooperative community relationships. This position helped to prepare Paul for his current vocational position, that of the first Director of FOCUS Pittsburgh and CEO of FOCUS Pittsburgh Health Center.

FOCUS stands for Fellowship of Orthodox Christians United to Serve. It also stands for Food, Occupation, Clothing, Understanding, and Shelter, the different facets of support provided by FOCUS. FOCUS is the community mission "arm" of the Orthodox Christian church in North America. "It is an organization that helps me to express both the social justice and spiritual components of myself." FOCUS provides community services (including health and social services) with care, kindness, equality, and stability. Every single service that they provide, is provided for free. To Paul, it is the perfect setting in which to show the love of Christ to the disenfranchised of the area: single parents, homeless and at-risk youth that live in the surrounding neighborhood, the Hill District of Pittsburgh. Paul lives with his new wife Christina in that neighborhood.

"While I was still in seminary, I had long conversations with younger priests who asked me "how" I would make such a ministry work. I felt that the Holy Spirit was calling me to Pittsburgh for a very specific goal and ministry, and told them that it wasn't my business to make it happen, but God's business."

Within five months after Paul's graduation from seminary, two groups of Pittsburgh Orthodox Christians helped Paul to get together the seed money to launch FOCUS Pittsburgh: a group of women who organized a fundraiser for the summer of 2010, and Theodora Polamalu, the wife of a local NFL star who talked to her contacts and to local clergy about investing in a needs-based project in the Hill District. There were also detractors, people who thought that Paul wouldn't be able to pull off the organization and funding of FOCUS Pittsburgh. There was skepticism around whether it could be done, whether it should be done, whether it could be successful and so on. "I knew that the need for this organization was so strong that God would make it happen, so I didn't worry about the naysayers. I had meetings with public officials, foundation officers, corporations and local religious leaders to hear what they had to say, so that they would know that they had input and influence in how this center was developed." By the winter of 2010, the development of FOCUS Pittsburgh was well under way, and Paul was in the Moving Forward phase of Fisher's Process.

The financial support from corporate and individual philanthropists, and the community support has been overwhelming to Paul. Once he was able to show local community leaders that he was very invested in the development of FOCUS Pittsburgh and would see things through, he met with key Pittsburgh philanthropists, which included conversations about the community center being a warm, welcoming, familiar place that wouldn't be too fancy or intimidating. "I had to help them see that if the center resembled a Starbucks or a luxurious bed & breakfast, that our neighbors wouldn't want to be there. I also told them that we always need more volunteers, and would be grateful for any assistance that we could have in that area."

In some ways, Paul's responsibilities never really end. Because Paul and his wife live in the neighborhood that they work in, their personal and professional lives overlap each other. The ministry at FOCUS is not as structured, which is something that Paul lost when he left the military and corporate settings behind him: clear, strong boundaries and structures between his professional and work lives. Paul is now required to exercise more patience, compassion, and empathy than in either of his other vocational paths, and there are very few "perks" that would be admired by any businessman looking at his ministry. But he has left other things behind, which he realized he would have had to embrace if he had stayed in the business world: "The FACADE of life! That lie that you are keeping it 100% 'together', 100% of the time. I have experienced an authentic, personal brokenness when looking at all of the needs of the people around me, and have been blessed by the authentic struggles and suffering that I am now a part of."

To have a good work/life balance, Paul has a couple of hobbies, including golf and reading Civil War novels. He spends quality time with his wife, his family members, and friends. As Paul waited for his ordination, he has some advice for others who are discerning a call to a priestly vocation: "Do not fear the Cross. A life of ministry will be a life of self-sacrifice, struggle and suffering (others' and your own). But the pain of the Cross cannot be separated from the joy of the Resurrection of Jesus. You will be filled with a special joy if you decide to embark on the journey of religious vocations."

Emily Sutton: Cumulative Damage But Moving On

Emily Sutton, age 34, is a pretty, tall woman with long wavy hair and cute wire-rimmed glasses. She meets me in a coffee shop in the deep North Hills, about 35 minutes from downtown Pittsburgh. Her open and expressive face mirrors her changing emotions, and she speaks fast and emotionally about her current foray off from her original vocational path.

For Emily, working for nine years with unpredictable clients and a hostile manager was a lesson in cumulative damage. Her position as a counselor in a residential home for at-risk teens had become physically dangerous, emotionally draining, and mentally exhausting. "What don't I miss about that job? The toxic work environment with management who used my job description to prevent me from getting increases in pay; the daily stress of working with burned-out coworkers and volatile clients; the injuries I sustained from violent teenagers. I loved the kids that I worked with, but the salary I was getting didn't make up for all the deficits of the job."

B.F. Skinner's writing on problem solving describes the process as "any behavior which, through the manipulation of variables, makes the appearance of a solution more probable" (Skinner, 1953). He describes an atmosphere in which a problem is solved, is one in which the person observes their own reaction to negative stimuli and decides based on those responses. Emily's descriptions of experiencing stress, exhaustion, disappointment and anger over the actions of management, and pain from the injuries caused by volatile clients, all point to self-awareness that negative stimuli had reached a point at which Emily was no longer able to maintain internal justification for staying in her job. Emily had passed through the Disillusionment stage of Fisher's Process, and was in the Hostility stage by the time she considered leaving her counseling position.

Emily had a decision before her, and she made her decision based on what was best for her overall health. She resigned her position at the residential facility, increased her part-time waitressing to full-time, and enrolled herself in college in the fall of 2013. Although Emily has a master's degree in Counseling and Psychology, and wanted to stay in a helping profession, she was burned out on social service work. She met with a nursing school admissions counselor and her therapist regarding her decision, and figured out that she needed some core classes before applying to nursing school. She will find out in April of 2015 whether she has been accepted to nursing school; if she is, will start full-time nursing curriculum in the fall of that year.

To fulfill this goal, Emily had to make difficult decisions regarding her home life: she couldn't work at waitressing and still pay all her bills (including her student loans), so she moved home with her parents and now commutes to her job and to classes in the North Hills of Pittsburgh. Her parents were very supportive of her decision to leave the counseling job, as was a man she was currently dating, and her close friends. Her landlord, on the other hand, made it difficult to leave her lease obligation, and there were shared utilities in the home, which made it difficult to tell whether Emily owed as much as her landlord requested from her. There is a financial "hangover" from that time that Emily is still attempting to catch up with.

Emily is attempting to get back into a scholarly frame of mind. It has been so many years since she was a full-time college student that she struggles with the transition: "I have more going on emotionally and mentally compared to when I was a freshman; I am more mature now, but my life - and its problems - are bigger and more complex. I have a lot of close girlfriends, and their issues (and my support of them) take up more emotional and mental space than they used to."

Emily had a wide base of support for her decision to leave her counseling job, but it's going to take time for her to get used to her new life. "My identity is in flux; I still don't feel comfortable that people see that I am a waitress, and wrongly deduce certain things about me. Many of my friends who are waiters and waitresses feel the same way, that people have negative perceptions of wait staff, and their decisions; but that's other people's loss, I guess, if they don't want to get to know us and who we really are." Emily's therapist has been a touchstone for her through this whole process. "My therapist helped me to see that this decision was thought through, that it wasn't an emotional choice but a valid, solid choice. Right after I resigned from my job, fear set in, and she helped me work through that. She also helped me to explore educational choices besides the nursing school option."

Emily wishes that she would have been more aware of how much money was needed to make this vocational transition. There were benefits to her old job that she misses, such as working with teens, the salary and other perks, like paid insurance. She has some coping skills to deal with her anxiety and stress in this new life, such as socializing with friends at work, smoking, and enjoying good food. Emily is still working through different types of study habits, to see which ones work best for her situation. Her advice to anyone who is facing a total vocational overhaul is to "think about what you want, and then what you have to do, to make it happen smoothly. If you are confident in your decision, then the identity shift will eventually happen on its own."

Robin Stanton: When The Going Gets Tough...

Robin Stanton is a pretty woman, short in stature with grey/green/blue eyes that change color depending on her mood. Her strong attitude and straightforward conversational style make the time pass quickly, and she's no lightweight; the trials she has borne for the sake of independence would give a strong man pause.

Robin never imagined how quickly her life could change, practically overnight. In 2007, pregnant with her second child, she discovered that her husband had been unfaithful and made the heartbreaking decision to seek a divorce. Eight years later, she now looks on that time and sees how fast everything fell into place, and has no regrets: "Everything in the universe has its timing, and with the support and help of my parents, everything fell into place." At the time, Robin was working with a consulting company in the field of affiliate marketing. She was making good money and was comfortable in her job, but knew that she would need the assistance of her parents in order for her children to receive the best care possible, and to have a stable home life. "I had heart and blood pressure issues during the pregnancy, and I believe that was because of the stress of being in a falling-apart marriage, but it was also from my own stubbornness."

Robin decided to move into her parents' house in Morgantown, PA, which was about two hours away from her husband. She had always seen her parents as her closest allies and her personal cheerleaders, and not only because she is an only child. Her mom and dad have always been communicative and supportive, and their response to Robin's separation was no different. Robin had some self-reflecting to do, and home was the best place in which to do it. "I now look back and recognize 'red flags' during our dating period, as we had a cycle of breakups between 2002 and 2007, and then we got married in January of 2007" but by October 2007 they were officially divorced. Robin's ex-husband had numerous character flaws, not the least of which was that he was sure that Robin wouldn't break up with him after discovering the infidelity. He was upset that Robin moved away with their older daughter while pregnant, and so responded to that "inconvenient" situation by digging in his heels and expecting Robin to facilitate visitations with the older daughter, who was just starting kindergarten when the couple separated.

In response to that unreasonable expectation, Robin dug in her own heels: "I didn't want to make this easier on him; he was the one who had cheated, I was the one who had to move in with my parents in order to have a good life with my daughters, and I thought he should be willing to inconvenience himself a little more in order to see our kids." There were minimal financial repercussions from the divorce, at least for Robin and the kids, because of the higher salary that Robin was making. Robin found herself a newly single parent as her ex-husband's involvement with the girls quickly faded and eventually became nonexistent.

Financially there wasn't an impact, but personally, there were some costs to moving in with her parents. "I have great parents, we have a good relationship, but I think I stayed with them too long - five years!" Robin maintained relationships with her friends where she had grown up, and when at a critical juncture in her career, made the decision to move to Pittsburgh, PA instead of a southern state. "In 2012, I had some big decisions to make, and decided that I would rather start over in my hometown rather than take the girls to a completely unknown city."

Robin moved with her girls back to the Pittsburgh area in 2012, and settled into a new normal. Her older daughter was in elementary and her younger daughter was in preschool. Robin operated out of a home office in her new home and was available for school events and when the children were home sick from school. She reconnected with old friends, and made new ones.

Robin even started a new hobby - baking. This new skill came into play in January of 2015, when the affiliate marketing company she remotely worked for collapsed. Although she only had a week's heads up, Robin says "I didn't take it personally. Affiliate marketing has served me well as a career, giving me flexibility and a good salary. But it has become a cutthroat business, that change happened in 2013 but it **really** became noticeable by November of 2014." Robin moved quickly through the stages of Fear, Denial and Depression in Fisher's Process, and arrived at Gradual Acceptance.

Robin had some choices to make: stay in the same cutthroat business, whose future was uncertain, or take her vocational life in a completely different direction? Robin decided to take a big risk, and turned her baking hobby into a business opportunity. She had gotten high praise from friends and family regarding the quality of her baked products, but wasn't sure whether she had a good shot at making a go of a small, homestyle bakery business.

Robin researched the standards and certifications needed. She began the journey by visiting an Open House at the Pittsburgh Public Market, where she was introduced to the manager and was walked through the steps to get the needed certifications for food distribution. Robin already had the marketing angle covered, her previous career had totally prepared her for that, but wasn't aware what other angles needed to be covered until late in January of 2015. That is when she took the day-long training for her Food Certification license. It had only been a few weeks since she was laid off from her marketing position, but Robin felt truly comfortable "forging ahead and being the master of my own destiny."

After that training, Robin held her breath as she waited for the results of her Food Certification license tests, and was so excited when she passed! She now has her local license, her state and county permits. Her Food Certification is good for three years, at which time she will have to re-test, but she doesn't see that as a barrier. "I am having so much fun! It was a little scary at first, being my own boss and drawing on my personal money and savings so that Get Mo' Muffins could be up and running, but this is a new adventure! I make my own schedule, I make good products and can't wait to introduce them to the public. I have a lot to learn, but my marketing background gave me a good start, and I have a bachelor degree in Business Science, so I think that will cover it." Robin is squarely in the Moving Forward stage of Fisher's Process, in that she believes that this new vocational path can work, and be good.

Robin credits her children (taste testers), her parents (moral support and financial support) and her circumstances (being laid off) for launching her into this new career. She also received a lot of advice and mentoring from the manager of the Pittsburgh Public Market, where Robin rents prep, oven and storage areas to create her product line (she quickly grew out of the home kitchen). That mentoring helped Robin to quickly feel adjusted and confident in her new vocation. She is happier being a small business owner because she gets to see all the urban Pittsburgh neighborhoods, meet new people, network with other small business owners, and is responsible for steering her own career. Robin does enjoy promoting her new business, but "I don't like getting too much unsolicited advice from people. I'm trying to figure this out for myself, I am very independent and stubborn, and that's just how I operate."

Robin doesn't miss her old career, per se, but does miss some of the friends that she had in that business and the national traveling that she got to do with that position. She doesn't miss the high level of stress, nor the frequent industry changes with which she was expected to keep up.

Robin copes with stress by hanging out with friends, exercising sometimes, and hanging out with her two girls. "If the stress gets to be too much, I tend to withdraw and drop off the social radar, so I'm trying not to do that."

Robin's next step is to build brand recognition for Get Mo' Muffins and to keep the business going until at least her younger daughter graduates from high school (in ten years). She is working on her business plan, promoting her business, and making changes as necessary. She has also incorporated her children into the business by having them accompany her when she does food production and deliveries.

Robin tweaked her business plan recently, because she was spending more money on the rental of a product table at the Market than she was making back in sales, and that was consistently the case, so she stopped selling her products at that venue. She has since added two wholesale order locations, three local farmers markets, and some pop-up bakery days are scheduled. "I also arranged to have a snack booth on location at my girls' performing arts center every Saturday." Robin shows a great deal of initiative, creativity and flexibility in her business approach, and those skills ensure that she gets enough sales to continue this vocational path. Her passion, work ethic, and determination are obvious to anyone who sees her at work, and her enthusiasm for her products is inspiring! You could never tell that two situations that would seem to be most devastating to identity - the loss of a spouse through divorce, and the loss of a job by layoffs - have helped to center and focus Robin's vocational identity.

"My advice to others is to keep trying until you find something that you love. Don't give up! Do what makes you happy, it's okay to make yourself happy. Also: trust your intuition, your gut instinct."

Christina Brussalis: 9/11, And Becoming A Mother

Christina Brussalis welcomes me to her well-appointed home in the South Hills of Pittsburgh, moving boxes and bare counters a testament to her life in flux. "I'm so sorry the timing isn't great, but we are in the middle of moving to the North Hills!" she graciously explains, guiding her little girl to the table for snack (while listening intently to the baby monitor to make sure her baby boy is settled into his nap). Life with three children can be hectic anyway, as her oldest child is 14 and involved in school and social activities, and her husband's professional career is demanding. Christina sets us at the dining room table, serves coffee, and then settles in while feeding snacks to her daughter.

"What happened on September 11, 2001 marked a critical career decision point for me. It had already been rather difficult in Washington D.C. for me as a new single mom, trying to find consistent daycare for my 4-month-old and finding a satisfying work/life balance. I had friends and family coming to help with my daughter, because there were no day care slots available near my home and work. I was in a challenging and stressful career as the Confidential Assistant for the Assistant Secretary of Defense. I had been in Washington D.C. for 4.5 years, including my internship, and was just "over it": the long work days, the limited time with my new baby, the long commute from my home in the suburbs that I shared with my cousin. And then 9/11 happened. I was in the Pentagon that day."

The 9/11 terrorists used four planes in three locations to attack the World Trade Center in Manhattan, New York City; the Pentagon in Washington D.C.; and a field in Pennsylvania (that plane was assumed to be headed back towards the east coast to attack the White House when civilian passengers fought the terrorists and forced the plane to the ground in time to avert a larger-scale tragedy). Civilians, rescue service personnel, military personnel and police in all three locations woke up that morning assuming life would be business as usual. By 10:03 a.m., when Flight 93 crashed into a field in Shanksville, Pennsylvania, life in America was forever changed.

For Christina, the immediate career impact occurred in workplace structure: all Pentagon personnel were immediately evacuated to other locations for safety, but then for functional reasons as well. The Pentagon building's structure had to be stabilized and inspected, and in the following week, a memo was sent out that pregnant and nursing moms shouldn't return to the Pentagon because of health concerns related to building materials being exposed by the plane's impact. As a nursing mom, Christina was transferred to the American Forces Information Services building. "Work in that environment was hectic and disconnected from the rest of the team, and I had already decided that I was going to resign from my position with the Assistant Secretary. The travel required to perform my position was largely unrealistic for the needs of my little family." Prior to 9/11, she had been looking for civilian positions with the military, and corporate jobs in Washington D.C., without finding the perfect fit (an appropriate salary for her situation, and an amenable office location). Christina had also searched for jobs in the Pittsburgh area and in Akron, Ohio, in the fields of Public Relations, Media, and

Marketing, with no luck. Christina was in the Disillusionment Stage of Fisher's Process, and the 9/11 crisis at work helped to push her towards drastic changes in her career and lifestyle.

Christina made the decision to resign her position at the Pentagon, and to return home to live with her parents in rural New Castle, Pennsylvania. She looked for positions near her new home, spent time with her family, and took care of her daughter. "I was frequently in the first 6 months home; I felt caught between my old and new lives. I missed my friends in D.C., my social life there, and the exciting atmosphere, including the multicultural atmosphere, the museums, and the urban setting. I also hadn't fully adjusted to the huge changes that had happened from becoming a mom for the first time; I had some embarrassment at first over being a single mom, and was adjusting to making decisions for both of us, instead of just me." Christina had to make a conscious decision to mentally "release" her life in Washington which was sometimes difficult, because she was offered other Secretary positions after she had already returned to (and settled into) her life in New Castle: "I had to detangle my desire to return to my old life from my more realistic expectations, of how my life had actually changed since having my daughter," which included life in a small rural town with a slower pace of life, with a homogeneous population. By the summer of 2002, Christina's home and social life had fallen into a rhythm that she was comfortable with, and she was enjoying it.

Christina's job search yielded no success until September of 2002, when she secured a position as a substitute teacher in the local public school. Because her job was through the county's Intermediate Unit, she worked with elementary, middle, and high school children. She also secured a teaching position at a detention center (which was high security, and sometimes stressful).

"I had many people helping me during that time; my mother cared for my daughter full-time, my parents and extended family provided practical and emotional assistance, and many of my high school friends provided emotional and social support." In addition, Christina had made new friends in New Castle, friends in similar situations who helped her to feel normal, to laugh, and to relax. Christina had reached the Moving Forward Stage of Fisher's Process.

One of the aspects of her life in Washington D.C. that Christina really missed (and sought to fulfill again in New Castle) was involvement in political activity. "In 2004, I had the opportunity get involved in local politics in New Castle. That lead me to volunteer with a

Congressional hopeful, and it landed me my first big job in New Castle, as a Community Outreach Coordinator. I was working with a local District Attorney, and ended up volunteering for (future) Governor Ed Rendell's campaign."

Christina's mother was a real lifeline for her, caring for Christina's daughter until the start of kindergarten, giving her relationship and professional advice, and was very sympathetic about Christina's situation: "My mom had been in a similar situation with me, and only saw me on the weekends, when she would come home from her job in Washington D.C.! So she really knew how hard it was to find work/life balance in the capital, and was fully supportive of my move back home." She also encouraged Christina to have an active social life, to get out there, make friends and a new life in New Castle.

Christina's daughter, and their life together, really grounded her and helped her to come into her new "self." "Our relationship was unique, new to me, very fulfilling and created a lot of happiness for me. We socialized with my family and my mom's friends, eating Hungarian food and speaking Hungarian (both of which were a comfort for me). We spent time with other local moms and their children, which helped me to grow in confidence as a parent and as a woman."

In hindsight, Christina was able to see the benefits of leaving Washington D.C. behind: "Family life was too hard there. I felt alone in my new role as a young mom, and it was far from my parents and the rest of my family. It was too hectic and fast-paced for my new situation, especially having to travel without my baby."

Eventually Christina moved to Pittsburgh, remarried, and had two additional children. She worked with her husband's firm on an as-needed basis, and is currently a full-time stay at home mom. "I'm not sure what I'll do next, I'm too busy doing this! I probably have to figure out what my passion is, besides my family; and how that can translate into the next phase of my work life. I'm not sure when that will be, nor what the circumstances would have to entail (so there is nothing to really prepare for, per se)."

"Anyone who is in the situation that I was in? My advice is: make a plan. Network with anyone you have worked for, or with, over the years, and ask them for help and advice. Then you enlist people that you trust to help you make that transition. That preparation will help to make you feel more confident than I did moving back home, because you will have more in place to help you to succeed in your phase of life.

I learned a lot during that time in between my two jobs, but I wouldn't recommend that you take that same approach. It's very difficult."

Rob Jones: Blue Collar Kid Turned Executive Trainer

For Rob Jones, the idea of "diversity" has been constructed by corporate environments that think that by using cultural buzzwords, corporations can appear to be creating multicultural work environments. "All the while, these companies use hiring, firing, and promotion practices that have more to do with nepotism and cronyism than with true multicultural efforts." Rob has an established cynicism towards the "trend" of diversity, having observed from the inside-out (and then from the outside-in) these cyclical patterns of worrying more about appearances than with the reality of the inner workings of a corporation, especially when it comes to people of color.

Mr. Jones' parents (and their backgrounds) hold as much weight as his work experiences in shaping his understanding of corporations and "diversity." Rob's mother was a first generation Russian Jew who worked in childcare and then as a dietician. His father was part black, part Native American and a blue-collar worker who worked first in the steel industry and then in transportation services. "This rich ethnic heritage created both a well-rounded school of life, and an understanding that our family was cross-cultural, cross-racial, and cross-religious, and that we held both a richness and a responsibility in this world." Rob's parents were both activists during the 1960's and 70's, and throughout Rob's childhood their living room was the site of many civil rights gatherings. Civil rights giants such as Miriam McKeever, Paul Robeson, and Joan Baez were hosted by Rob's parents for speaking events. These impactful people and moments helped to shape Rob's identity as a person, and eventually led him to see that "diversity" is a manmade construct that helps companies to feel good about themselves, but that it is only training, hiring and promoting people of color as a matter of everyday occurrence that really counts for anything.

Rob knows that of which he speaks: by 2011, he had been through four mergers and acquisitions in the energy industry, and he was getting TIRED. "Tired of being expected to be a "Yes" man, tired of the nepotism and cross-pollination of hiring across energy industry lines, you know? 'Hey, can you give my son a job, he just graduated from college and doesn't want to work for me', that sort of thing. Tired of all the talk about diversity but watching qualified people of color getting passed up for promotion. So when the new President/CEO of the outside company had a personality and style that completely clashed with mine, I knew that I was no longer a good fit for the organization." As Senior Manager, Rob had the education, experience, and staying power to deal with another round of changes to corporate environment, policies and politics, "but I could read the writing on the wall." When Rob was offered a severance package in 2011 upon returning from family vacation, he took the offer and ran with it. "I figured, the energy field is becoming so diversified with natural gas, water, wind, oil, and even waste energy production, why should I wait out another time of adjustment and shake up in the company, not really knowing what was coming down the road?" Rob had sensed that he might be asked to leave the company because of his incompatibility with the new president, and had prepared his wife ahead of time. "But it's my belief that I am me, not the function that I perform at work. I have security in my identity as a person, and I accepted that I would be that person, no matter what job I moved to next. Whether or not I was going to get a new or better job, I believed that it was better to leave a hostile work environment than to stay and fight for something that I didn't even want to have." In other words, Rob had been in the Disillusionment Stage of Fisher's Transition Process for quite some time,

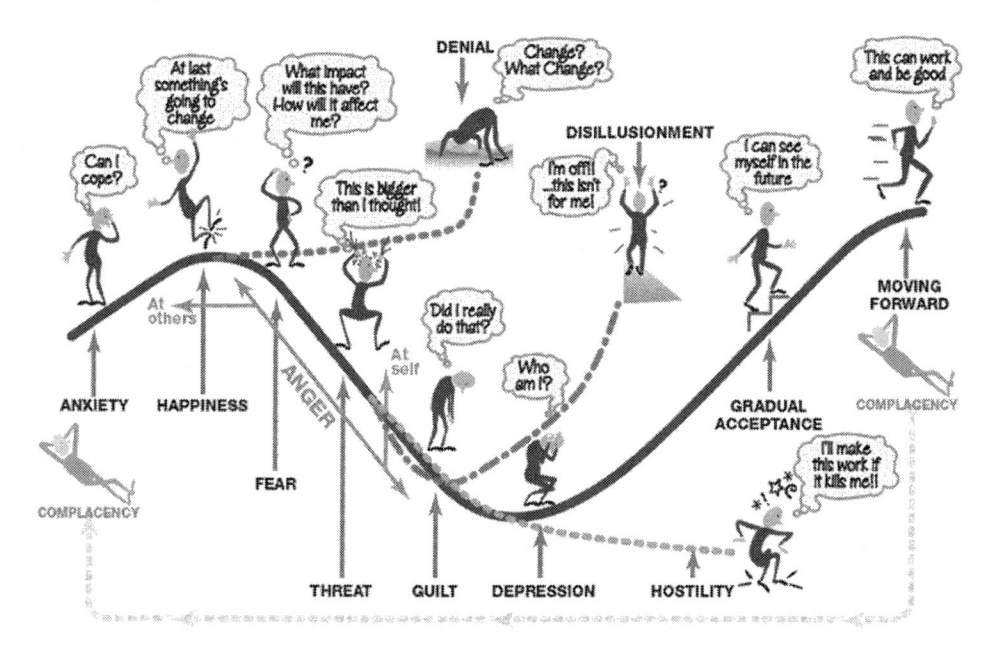

but had not been motivated to make a career change until the change was forced upon him. Many people in their 50's and 60's are reluctant to leave a stable job for an uncertain future, and Rob was no exception.

Being a self-determined (not "other"-determined) person, Rob got right to work on forging a new career path for himself. In the first six months after he separated from the energy company, Rob got moving on definitive steps towards re-entering the workforce. He did a lot of research on diversity and corporate environment and wrote two books, expanded his professional networking, and traveled to Canada to network there as well. He also discovered that some co-workers in his previous job were speaking negatively about him "but that didn't surprise me. You really find out who your friends and enemies are when you leave a job."

Realizing how extensive his professional network was, Rob decided on an unconventional next step. "I realized how brutal it is as a person of color and being close to 60 years old, how unrealistic it was to expect a corporate environment to make a place for me. So instead, I made a place for myself, and started my own company, called In Good Company." Rob had experience in training professionals, having coached executives with nonprofits, small businesses, and Chambers of Commerce since the 1980's.

"Having a degree in Human Resources Management, a degree in Information Systems, an MBA, and a Six Sigma Green Belt Certification, I was more than qualified to start my own Professional Executive Training Company. Now I train executives to have more balanced lives, to get the most out of their professional positions, and to acquire new skill sets. Much of what my training seminars touch on is Identity: who are you outside of what you do at work? I train them how you can affect something (the corporate culture) just by being a part of it, by asking the right questions, by getting rid of approaches that don't help yourself, your team, and your company.

"I teach them to recognize the difference between competition and cooperation. I demonstrate that business is more often about relationships than about the function of a company. My ultimate goal is to show executives how to capitalize on their most valuable asset: their employees. How can they most successfully utilize their team? How can they create a lasting, sustainable corporate environment that is streamlined and positive? How can they be more strategic in how they utilize their human assets?"

Rob's upbringing in a cross-cultural, -racial, -religious household most certainly began this idea in him, sunk itself into his character, his intellect, and his business values. His recognition was that underneath, we are all the same, and that each human represents so much potential as long as we are willing to look for it. Rob recognized that the only way to change, truly CHANGE, the corporate world, is from the outside in: to train executives, professionals, presidents and CEO's to have a more balanced corporate environment that cares for its employees, and to maximize their potential.

To that end, his advice is "Never let your thinking limit your perception of opportunity. You need to come to grips with the reality that there are structural barriers in place, ones that you will need to crawl under, dig under, or climb over. You may have to get 'small' again, concentrate on finer details and opportunities, in order to move into what you really want. If you fail: go ahead and cry for 20 seconds. And then get over it and MOVE ON."

Franne McNeal: To Be or Not To Be: Employees as Disposable Goods

For Franne McNeal, the foundation of self-confidence came from her top-notch education at a private school in Bryn Mawr, Pennsylvania. She was trained and taught by instructors who presupposed they were raising the next generation of women leaders, and much was expected from the students. Regardless, when Franne graduated from high school and entered Princeton University, she encountered many men who didn't believe that women could be business leaders. This furthered Franne's resolve to be just that, especially when she discovered that her Scottish last name created some confusion when she arrived at job interviews, because Franne is black. These two examples of prejudgment and expectation helped to propel Franne towards excellence in job performance and personal growth, because they opened her eyes to the type of employment bias for which she would need to prepare herself.

Franne first entered the corporate banking world after taking computer technology courses in the early 1990's. She began that leg of her career at PNC Bank in Pittsburgh, Pennsylvania as a contract computer services employee. She had worked the three previous years in various support positions in East Liberty, an urban neighborhood of Pittsburgh. The position at PNC Bank was a high-paying hourly contract position, and Franne enjoyed training the bank executives in computer skills. Eventually Franne was referred to the Teller Trainer Program at PNC Philadelphia.

"My experience of corporate banking was not a positive experience! There is a 'secret language' of corporate life, with all sorts of unspoken expectations, especially for women, especially for single women. In retrospect, I see that I was a threat to the male-dominated authority of my peers; I did not play the corporate side game of social bonding, such as golfing, ego-stroking, constant networking, or being mentored. There is a 1950's mentality in banking, that of powerful (mostly white) men who line female workers up behind them. It makes them feel powerful, to create a dynamic of subservience with these smart, educated women. I refused to buy into it; I loved my job and did not want anyone implying that I had advanced in my career due to my connections." Now that Franne is older and wiser, she also recognizes that the core mission of a corporate bank - "gobbling up small businesses as assets, refusing to see employees as valuable cogs in the machinery, viewing employees as both inconsequential and disposable" - did not match her personal view of what makes a business important to a community. Franne also delayed getting her master's degree in order to engage in the Teller Trainer Program, which she now sees as a mistake.

Franne believes that her refusal to give into internal corporate politics is what eventually derailed her progress at PNC Bank Philadelphia. "I lodged a complaint against a fellow employee, a white male. I was told by corporate (in Pittsburgh) to manage it myself, not to bother corporate with my complaint." And, sometime in the late 1990's, as Franne worked as a Vice President of PNC, PNC Philadelphia became the target of layoffs and firings. "The strong people were picked off first, like on the game Survivor. Friends of mine who were at the executive level in Human Resources, they were saying one thing and doing another: giving assurances that certain jobs were safe, but then laying off or firing those people."

"I put a final target on my back when, after 4.5 years of working at the executive level, I argued with Human Resources to not force a co-worker to fly to another city, just to be humiliated and fired. I was told, don't tell her she is being fired, or you will lose your job." During this time, Franne was in the Threat stage of Fisher's Process, and six months later, Franne was 'let go.' "I came to recognize that at PNC, the Human Resources department treated employees as disposable goods, to be acquired, consumed, and disposed of - or in the case of white males, to be recycled in other iterations in other departments. HR should have been investing in good employees, getting them additional training, identifying future leaders, etc. They never lived what they 'preached': Employees Come First!"

Franne experienced ambivalence during her transition out of that job: "My identity was in my work. I felt hurt, betrayed and angry, not the least of which had to do with that I was only SIX MONTHS from being vested, which would have made me eligible for a pension!" Franne was experiencing the stages of Depression and Disillusionment of Fisher's Process: "Who am I? Who am I outside of this job? What will happen now, what can I do?" Franne's experience was so negative that she decided to take some time off work, and so she distracted and psychologically renewed herself by volunteering with a summer program for youth in Philadelphia. Three months of sun, relating to youth, physical exercise, and busyness: it was a good experience, and an excellent counteraction to being fired. She also spent time with friends and family, professional associates and colleagues, talking about her experience and releasing her anger about being fired. That summer helped to move Franne to the Gradual Acceptance stage: "I can see myself in a different career, I can see myself in the future."

Franne also spent time in personal reflection and came to some conclusions about what she should have done differently: "I should have asked for protection from the female manager in the Philly office, to reduce the professional consequences of filing a complaint against the male employee. I would be less naive about what it means to be a smart, Masters-educated, black, single female in the corporate world. I would have recognized that one of my fellow female employees was working to help get me fired, and that she was not to be trusted. I recognize now that corporate environments have a mentality of sink-or-swim, not team identity and the encouragement to succeed."

In the autumn of 2001, Franne felt refreshed enough to tap into the membership of her professional association, the American Society for Training and Development. Via feedback from members, she decided to start a small business called HR Energy, through which she developed leadership training for entrepreneurs. "I saw a need, and met that need. Another bonus? Being my own boss." Franne was experiencing the Moving Forward stage: "This can work and be good!"

Franne headed up HR Energy from 2001 until 2006, and then decided to switch focus. She moved on to develop Significant Business Results, a business through which she serves clients by clarifying their business plans and results, and that helps businesses to focus on leadership development through cooperative plans. Additionally, 2006 was a significant year in the Philadelphia business scene, because there were massive numbers of layoffs and an uptick in suicides, especially among white male businessmen. "I witnessed firsthand that, conversely, minority employees were capable of regrouping from the corporate environment to small business, with self-owned identities. Black employees, specifically, were going on to create their own jobs or finding jobs that were more suited to their personal career goals."

Franne still owns Significant Business Results (SBR) today, more than ten years later. She has expanded her business acumen as a volunteer interviewer for a Philadelphia television show that highlights entrepreneurs. She also uses her master's in Business Administration in a unique way, as a Business Advisor in an academic environment, via a grant program. In that capacity, she is a member of a small team, and is not a manager, which helps her to further hone her team-building skills, which gives her more sympathy for the clients of SBR.

"I love my job! I don't plan to retire anytime soon, although I am eligible for retirement at age 62, which is only 6 years from now. I plan to keep going, to probably work part-time from age 67 to 75. Maybe at 75 I'll retire for real!"

Franne has additional goals for herself: she would like to teach at an accredited university such as Temple University, but would need a Ph.D. to be considered for that position. Franne is working online to achieve that goal within three years.

Franne's advice to others who have been laid off or fired? "Focus on what works. Ask questions: What will work next? What do I want more of? What don't I know? What is the subtlety that I am missing, in my career field?

Lastly, involve other people that you trust, ask them how you could avoid repeating the same mistakes. One good way to do that is to find a mentor in your chosen field, someone who speaks the 'language' of your career path."

Chapter 8:
Retirement Stories and Twilight Adventures

What does a "healthy" retirement look like? What is the difference between planned retirement, and an abrupt or involuntary end to your career in the twilight years? And how does retirement planning fit as a type of control over this stage in career life? All these questions, and more, come to the forefront when comparing and contrasting retirement stories. A few things become clear:
- When retirement is well-planned and voluntary, the adjustment feels milder, more positive, and more like a controlled descent than a crash-and-burn end to your career; and perceptions of satisfaction are higher (Szinovacz & Davey, 2005).
- When retirement is unexpected and involuntary, physical health is negatively affected, depression rates increase, and personal well-being takes a downturn (Hershey & Henkens, 2013).

- For those who engage in non-career activities once retired (such as civic engagement, volunteering, or a vigorous hobby), their perception of the state of retirement will be largely positive (Hershey & Henkens, 2013).
- For those who hadn't anticipated health declines and other age-related correlations after retirement, their perception of retirement will be (at least initially) largely negative (Hershey & Henkens, 2013).
- Both health limitations and job displacement lead to increased perceptions of forced retirement (Szinovacz & Davey, 2005).

To better illustrate the dynamics of forced retirement, here's the story of Pat Mahon:

Pat Mahon: Transformation Project? Or Nasty Surprise?

Pat Mahon welcomes me to his spacious home near Greentree Road, a major throughway near the highway into downtown Pittsburgh. At first his nervousness appears to be from having a stranger in his home, but then Pat explains that he has a lot of strong emotions around his forced retirement (anger, fear, disappointment and uncertainty about the future). His reactions mirror that of many forced-retirees around America who collect unemployment while they go through the motions of taking stock of what they have saved up, revising their spending patterns, and beginning a job search (a requirement of collecting unemployment) at an age when many of their peers are retiring (Brandon, 2011).

After more than 40 years as a contract specialist in banking, Pat Mahon already knew that large corporations often consolidate positions to decrease operating expenses and that they always prioritize the bottom line: money. What Pat, aged 63, didn't anticipate was being forced into early retirement because of BNY Mellon's new CEO's "Transformation Project", and being replaced by someone who had no experience in the specific aspects of his field. "They didn't give me enough time to properly train my replacement, to bridge the knowledge gaps for her; she didn't even get hired into my position until three weeks before I had to leave, even though they gave me six months' notice of the layoff."

This and other questionable layoff details left Pat scratching his head: "They told me that I could apply for three other positions, and then when I did that, didn't even get back to me to schedule interviews. They could have offered me a lower-paying position so that I could work to my planned retirement date, and paid me less while still having the advantage of the wisdom that I have after so many years in my field. It just doesn't make good business sense."

Pat took as much time as he could to train his successor during the three weeks of overlapping employment, showing her the global nature of what he had done in the last eight and a half years at BNY Mellon. He simply didn't have time in that time to show her the finer distinctions of his position, which included retirement plan negotiations and other complex interactions with outside clients. "I sympathized with her, and felt bad that she might feel lost after I was gone; I left her a large file cabinet of closed projects so that she might have project references when dealing with the same companies in the future. I also told her about upcoming projects and what the negotiations might entail."

Pat's last day of work was in July of 2014. He has taken time since then to process through the feelings of disappointment, betrayal and confusion that the layoff created. "I had survived two significant layoffs in 2007 and 2008, and they weren't even going to let me interview for the three positions that were open, or to give me an explanation for that? I felt that this was an obvious case of age discrimination, but what would I have gained by pursuing a lawsuit? That would probably just be lost time, money and energy. I feel that management was fairly disconnected from the impact of their decisions, and didn't look at any of my 360 Performance Reviews while they were making the decision; I had great performance review scores." Pat is in the Depression stage of Fisher's Process: he is uncertain as to what the future holds, and what his place in that future will look like.

Pat's wife and three grown daughters have been a great support during this adjustment period, and Pat's wife has even told him that he is more relaxed than she has ever seen him. Even having to search for a job while on unemployment leaves him less stressed than he was at his previous position: "I had a lot of responsibility, and dealing with seven-figure accounts can leave you tense and stressed out. My wife really wants me to retire, she really likes how relaxed I am right now, and I am getting home projects done that I have put off. The truth is: if BNY doesn't want me anymore, I don't want to be there."

Though Pat recognizes those things to be true, he still feels that he is letting his family down by not sticking to the original plan, which was to work for three more years and bank all that money for future needs. "My wife works at Carlow University, but she really doesn't make enough on her own to support our lifestyle. I have been the main breadwinner all along, and it feels strange to not be providing for my family." After thoroughly reviewing their savings and retirement plans, he discovered that financially they will be fine, and that helped to allay some of his fears.

Although Pat's "new normal" still feels strange to him (and he misses some of his work friends and customers), he has used his newfound free time to work on house projects and spend quality time with his family. He has seen other friends retire and do well when they find part-time jobs that are fun or satisfying, or get out of the house and volunteer for various organizations. Retirement doesn't have to be fallow ground, it can be refreshing, and "you are your own boss", after all.

James Hilts: Transitions And Life Lessons

For James (Jim) Hilts, age 69, two career transitions stand out in his mind: one for the fresh start it afforded his adult life, the other for a continuing attempt to adjust that retirement represents.

After high school, two difficult years at the University of Buffalo, and the death of his mother, Jim decided to enroll at Niagara County Community College. He did excellently there, even making the Dean's List, and decided to re-apply to the University and was accepted. Jim was doing poorly again by the spring of 1967; he entered the Guilt stage of Fisher's Process, as things had not turned out the way that he had expected them to at the University. "And by that time, the Vietnam War was ramping up, so I knew that by leaving the university, I was categorizing myself 1A (a code that means that I was available for unrestricted military service)."

Instead of waiting to be drafted, he volunteered himself and was assigned to the Army's 1st Air Cavalry. Jim did basic training at Fort Dix in New Jersey, attended radio school, and was assigned as a radio teletype technician at Fort Gordon, Georgia. "By March of 1968, I was deployed to Vietnam. Within eight months, I was promoted from buck sergeant to duty sergeant and was reassigned to a signal battalion. There was a mortar attack on my encampment during this time, which caused me to go into shock the next morning; I required a shot of epinephrine to my heart to recover."

By March of 1969 he had been awarded the Bronze Star Medal, which is awarded for heroic or meritorious conduct during wartime. Jim had fulfilled his year of combat, and so was flown from Vietnam back to the United States. "Our flight arrived in Fort Lewis (in Washington State) in the middle of the night. There was no one to greet us, and we were delivered to unheated barracks and expected to make a go of it. It was pretty anticlimactic." Jim experienced an accelerated version of the Disillusionment and Depression stages of Fisher's Process:

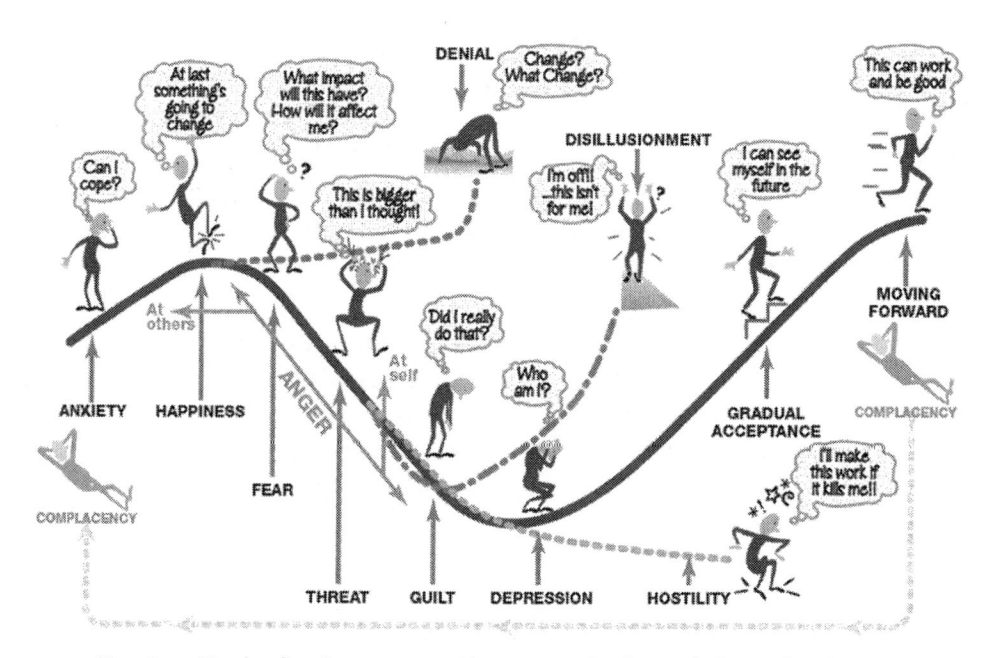

[Figure: Fisher's Process of Transition curve, showing stages from Anxiety, Happiness, Fear, Threat, Guilt, Depression, Hostility, Gradual Acceptance, Moving Forward, to Complacency, with thought bubbles including "Can I cope?", "At last something's going to change", "What impact will this have? How will it affect me?", "Denial — Change? What Change?", "This is bigger than I thought!", "I'm off! ...this isn't for me!", "Did I really do that?", "Who am I?", "I can see myself in the future", "This can work and be good", "I'll make this work if it kills me!!"]

During Jim's deployment, Christine (a friend from high school) was extremely beneficial as a touchstone. She wrote letters to him often, and they shared the details of their lives and became closer than friends. When Jim returned stateside, he pursued courtship with Chris and they were married soon afterwards. "I kept busy working various manufacturing jobs and making a life with Chris, and because of my upbringing in a military family, experienced very little negative effects from my wartime experiences." The one time he can remember having a reaction that was probably related to his war service was when an assembly line at the plant ground to a halt; he said that "it made so much noise that I automatically hit the deck."

Jim has heard many stories of men who experienced great difficulty adjusting to civilian life after the Vietnam War but thankfully, he was spared from such experiences. It seems that Jim was already in the Moving Forward stage of Fisher's Process as he adjusted to work life back in the United States. It may be that Jim's experience of camaraderie, respect, and soldierly duty and identity were so ingrained because of the pre-existing military identity of his family, and that he just absorbed his wartime experiences as normative and par for the course.

Jim's adjustment to retired life has been vastly different. After returning from the Vietnam War and marrying Chris, Jim worked at various manufacturing positions and finished his bachelor's degree. Jim and Chris started a family, moved to the Pittsburgh area and had three children. "And eventually I achieved my master's in Civil Engineering and started my own engineering firm, Kingsway Engineering, which I owned for 18 years."

Owning his own business was very stressful but rewarding. There were positive AND negative effects of ownership, both professionally and personally. "Retiring meant being able to let go of toxic people whom I had ties to because of my work; it was something I looked forward to." To help alleviate some of Jim's work stress, his wife Chris worked for his business from 2008 until his retirement in January of 2014. Part of her reasoning came from wanting to support Jim in his business and be his helpmate, part of it came from wanting a break on their health insurance. Jim and Chris shared Jim's salary, so that his business wouldn't experience financial difficulties from providing an extra salary for Chris.

Since retiring, Jim says "It's like a burden has been lifted from my shoulders, but I also feel a bit lost." He is in the Depression stage of Fisher's Process: the lack of structure in his daily schedule feels strange after so many years of regular and regimented work schedules. Kingsway had 65 regular and unique customers, so Jim's business was always busy, always stressful. The lack of that is something that Jim still has to get used to, but Chris welcomes the loosening of their schedules. There is more time to travel to see their children and grandchildren, more time to devote to church activities, more time to spend together as a couple and in support of each other. "There is a deepening to our marriage (and our faith) that we now have the time to appreciate and take notice of."

Jim's struggle to accept his new identity as retiree is something he regularly thinks and prays about; he recognizes that he is struggling with the many losses associated with retirement and other life changes. Jim is now somewhere between the stages of Depression and Gradual Acceptance in Fisher's Process. Jim and Chris recently downsized to a smaller house, and sold the home where they had raised their children and hosted many social and prayer group activities. This significant change in living environment also contributes to Jim's occasional feeling of disorientation.

"My faith (my personal relationship with God) and my wife Chris are my two biggest supports" during this awkward transition to retired life. He doesn't feel quite ready to give anyone advice on how to transition easily to retirement, but upon reflection, it may have been useful to him to find another retiree who could have mentored him through the process. Jim does acknowledge that activities such as hobbies and personal pursuits (he is considering getting back into finishing a stained-glass project that he began some years ago) will be a useful addition to retired life.

Diane Colson: From Divorcee to Retiree to Volunteer

Diane Colson, age 66, had a plan for retirement: her ideal plan was to retire at age 60, then to travel the country (the world?) with her second husband. But having married young, become a mom to two boys, and then divorced and remarried (all while juggling family life, moving across the country, and working), she was accustomed to bouncing back from unanticipated obstacles and even "You can't do that!" from some relatives. Diane's early divorce had set her on the path to self-reliance: she was determined to not depend on someone else's good will or financial provision ever again.

So, "I wasn't emotionally prepared for a second divorce, but I was definitely financially able to provide for myself and rely on myself." In June 2006, Diane and her second husband separated; for five years they struggled and attempted reconciliation, and then jointly filed for divorce in 2011. One of the points of contention during the separation and mediation was the ability to retire early: "Now I was looking at sole ownership of the house, all the financial responsibilities of that; whether I could actually afford to retire, because our financial planning had figured on two retirement incomes; how to fairly split our assets, and so on. Also, there was this: I had worked the graveyard shift as a

Certified Nurse's Assistant for 7 years, from 1979-86 while my husband went to school full-time and worked part-time. That degree set him up to make a very good wage; mine isn't low, per se, but I have a diploma from Minneapolis Business College and work as an accountant." Indeed, in economists' terms, there is hardly ever what is considered a 'financially fair' divorce. People plan their lives as if they will always be together, and so there is a natural living standard differential when the couple divorces, as it is cheaper for two people to live together than to divorce (Kotlikoff, 2015).

Divorce as the breaking of a social contract is one thing; divorce as the breaking of a financial contract is quite another. In the wake of a divorce, income drops 26% in households headed by women vs. 15% in households headed by men (Landers, 2017). Additionally, women live longer than men, are more likely to be custodial parents of minor children, and more likely to lose out by a common legal tactic (stretching out the settlement period so that the woman will "cave" and agree to less than she legally deserves) (Landers, 2017).

In addition to scrambling to financially reframe her future (including moving the timeline of her retirement), Diane was also faced with grieving the loss of her husband and other losses that followed: friends who sided with her husband in the divorce, social activities with couple friends, stability in her social life, and a shift in her sense of self. Diane recognizes that she experienced depression during (and after) her divorce, and that made it more difficult to think about the future, particularly how her retirement would be structurally and financially affected by the loss of her husband's income. She was in the stages of Depression and Hostility of Fisher's Process.

Nevertheless, Diane decided to retire in 2015 at the age of 62. She consulted with her financial advisor, whom she had an account with for 15 years (and alongside the stress of her company being sold twice), decided that retirement should commence as she had previously planned. An additional impetus was that her work building had bad air quality due to shared venting with a manufacturing facility, and she needed to consider its health impact. It wouldn't have made sense for her to start over in a different company, which would have increased her stress and possibly decreased her income.

Diane arranged her transition plan at work, training the receptionist (who was in accounting college) and setting in motion the retirement paperwork through Social Security. Also, the home in which she had raised her family had become too burdensome and was starting to need costly repairs and replacement. "I made a budget and plan for completing home improvements and repairs, with the goal of selling my home and starting my retirement in something smaller and more manageable." During this time, she looked for advice and support from two of her friends who had experienced recent, late-in-life divorces. She kept in constant contact with a friend who lived across the state, and sought advice from friends and relatives on Medicare plans. "I began to discover how complicated the supplemental health and prescription insurance process is, and how much retirees must pay out-of-pocket to maintain proper health coverage, and that Obamacare had raised the costs of both individual and company health coverage."

After retirement, Diane discovered a job at which she could work only one day a week which would cover her health insurance costs and other incidentals. After two years there, she resigned her position, sold her home and signed on for a volunteer position in the Parks Department in the Outer Banks of North Carolina. She bought a recreational vehicle in which she could live, and it was big enough to tow her car. Diane left Wisconsin in April of 2017, spent some time with relatives in Pennsylvania, and traveled to her volunteer assignment.

"Hindsight being 20/20, I believe that a smarter approach would have been selling my house directly after the divorce, which would have made me more money, because the housing recession hit Wisconsin in recent years. Also, I should have waited to retire until 65, which would have let me set aside more savings, but I had good reasons at the time. That's all the advice I can give. Every person's situation is different."

Lou Cosentino: Providence, not Coincidence

Lou Cosentino, age 70, has experienced a lifetime of almost unbelievable providential circumstances. Each vocational change has come from an already-existing relationship or connection; if we were to look at the chain of events from above, it would look like a row of dominoes laid out in a perfect pattern. Even his retirement, though not self-driven, created a catalyst for fulfillment that Lou could not have predicted. And Lou's friendly demeanor and personality reflect wisdom and positivity that have driven and shaped each one of his steps along the way.

"I grew up in an Italian immigrant family, and my parents were driven by hard work and community connection." The values instilled in Lou by his father ranged from loyalty to high work ethic to daily structure, and those values helped Lou to forge his own vocational path, especially after he decided that he did NOT want to take on the family business. Lou's dad had built a business from the ground up, designing and fabricating stainless steel kitchen equipment, but it didn't interest Lou enough to sacrifice his own vocational aspirations. And so Lou chose to study economics at the University of Pittsburgh; he quickly ascertained that the curriculum was too rigid for his liking, and switched his major to business education.

"Getting my bachelor's degree took ten years, as I got married to my wife April, switched from the university to drafting school to get a more immediate and lucrative job, and then returned to night school at Pitt to finish my bachelor's degree."

As Lou embarked upon his new career, he attained positions in local Pittsburgh industry giants that ranged from Pittsburgh Des Moines Steel to Westinghouse, to Dravo to Keystone Diesel, to USAir to Bombardier. The vocational moves that he made came from two different, internal questions: "Am I happy?" and "Am I making enough money to support my family?"

Much of the time, Lou worked in the field of sales and service of people movers (mass transit systems, like you would use in an airport). "I prayed about each decision, and processed through each change in jobs." Lou's flexible personality contributed to an almost uncanny ability to let go of one vocational aspiration and attach to the next; he was a quick study and paid attention to management and business dealings. Lou assessed when to move on quickly from the Disillusionment stages to the Gradual Acceptance and Moving Forward stages of Fisher's Process, and took action to move on to another job opportunity.

Faith in God and a belief in providence play a big part in Lou's vocational life; each time a door was about to close, another one opened. Lou doesn't believe in coincidence, he believes in a personal God who is very interested in the small questions of life and how best to individually answer those questions for each person. He remembered three things that his Dad had repeated to Lou, over and over: "Always pay your bills. If you say you'll do something, do it or tell them why you can't. If anyone ever does you a favor, don't ever forget it." These tenets of loyalty, faithfulness to relationships, and responsibility helped to shape the way that Lou operated in both his professional and personal lives, and looking from the outside, a type of vocational karma took effect. As Lou consistently operated from a place of loyalty and honesty, his professional relationships stayed intact, even as he moved on to other jobs. And some of those same co-workers came into play later, and provided leads to other jobs along the way.

In July of 2010, at the age of 63, Lou was suddenly presented with the option for early retirement and he accepted the proposal. Lou had been working for Bombardier for some time and the company had started massive layoffs. Bombardier had replaced some American employees with their Canadian employees; the uncertainty had made Lou feel burnt-out. He officially retired in August of 2010, did home improvement projects for five months that he had been putting off, and then started volunteering at a local food bank in the spring of 2011.

Lou started to feel that his fallow time at home wasn't working for him, and shortly thereafter, saw someone he knew from 20 years ago working at an auto parts store as a delivery man. He asked him about the job, and it sounded appealing, so Lou applied for the open delivery position and was hired in May of 2012. He still gets several free days a week to tend to personal matters, and likes that the delivery job keeps him physically fit and gives him several structured days per week. He makes his own hours, gets to meet new customers, and enjoys driving around local towns.

Lou ponders on the advice given him by his friend Bill, who experienced a stroke and was forced to retire, but then reinvented himself as a hospital volunteer afterwards: "Do what you love, not what you have to do; make decisions on the particular needs of your family, not on money." That advice helped Lou to take more risks and to learn new things; he has also reaped many benefits from reading *What Color is Your Parachute?* by Richard Nelson Bolles (1970). The book helped him to shape his extracurricular life, including learning to play guitar in his 30's, which led him to play guitar for the folk group in his parish, which led to an introduction to Joe Negri (a local Pittsburgh legend) through a local Monsignor (elder in the Catholic church), which led to an introduction to Carl Apone (a Pittsburgh music critic), who encouraged Lou to become involved in fundraising for the Pittsburgh Symphony.

"All along the way, my wife April and our two daughters have supported me, both emotionally and prayerfully." Lou feels that his Christian faith and participation in church services have borne him up during uncertain times, especially during vocational transitions.

"Looking back at my life, I would say that it was providence, not coincidence, that shaped my career path."

Sharon Alberts: Sisyphus As A Nonprofit CEO

My minivan winds around hill after hill, cutting across main roads and then up into a typical southwestern Pennsylvania neighborhood, with parked cars on both sides of the street with room for only one car to pass through in either direction. A little girl wearing a tutu, t-shirt and Spiderman mask stares at me as I carefully fold in my driver's side mirror (a Pittsburgh must under these street conditions) and wave to her. She is holding a stick, and gently waves the stick at me, then disappears behind a line of garbage cans.

Sharon Alberts welcomes me into her modest brick home, offers me iced tea and we settle in at her antique dining table in the dining room. Sharon is in her 60's with short dark hair, talks fast (like a lot of other Pittsburghers), is intelligent and witty. She loves her husband, her foster son, and her cats fiercely, and her loyalty and devotion comes across when she speaks of any of them.

Regardless of the full and varied shape that her schedule takes nowadays, nothing in Sharon's life now can compare to the professional and emotional responsibility of her 25 years of employment as the CEO of a nonprofit residential agency in Pennsylvania. The agency provides and coordinates housing, life skills training and support, and advocacy for clients with mental health and cognitive issues. The clients receive support at three different housing levels: group homes, community residential (individual apartments with 24-hour staff, with or without roommates), and supportive independent living.

"Being the 'face' of an agency is sometimes exhausting, especially when trying to justify budgets and approaches to outside funding sources, including governmental agencies. I was ready to retire in 2010, but because of stock market trends, put off my decision so that my financial future would be more stable." Sharon was experiencing the Disillusionment and Depression stages of Fisher's Process. She gave notice to the agency's board of directors a year before she left, in the hopes that the year would give them time to find an in-house successor; the board had other ideas, and did a successful outside search for the next CEO. That year gave Sharon time to disentangle her identity from her role as CEO; like other nonprofit leaders, her heart and soul had been poured into the agency, and it was more than a job to her, it was truly a vocation.

For the next year, Sharon stayed on board as a consultant, and experienced the relief of being separated from the role of CEO, but still being able to help the agency shape its future. "I enjoyed that year as consultant; I made my own schedule and was able to enjoy the freedom of not working full-time." It was a little strange to be present in the company as the new CEO made impactful decisions, but Sharon dealt with that discomfort and relished the freedom of not being in the "hot seat" for once.

After a year as consultant, Sharon met with the CEO and asked her if she wanted to Sharon to continue in a consultant role, and the CEO agreed to that. For nine more months, Sharon worked with the board of directors and new CEO to develop a business Process so that there could be a for-profit aspect to the agency, so that those profits could then benefit and grow the non-profit side. "After not making progress in that plan, and having had some other uncomfortable situations arise, I decided it was best for me to separate permanently from the agency." According to Fisher's Personal Transition Curve, she was in the Disillusionment stage.

Sharon was glad she left when she did, because in the following six months, major members of her original leadership team were "let go" as their positions were eliminated to save money. Also, huge changes were made to the infrastructure and functions of the agency; that was hard for Sharon to hear about because of her long-term professional and personal investment in the agency's success.

"I do sometimes miss the excitement of my CEO position, because I was in the position to effect change and growth within the agency." She also liked the challenges of managing agency budgets and mediating relational difficulties between the leadership, supervisory, and direct care staff levels. She now uses those transferable skills as her church board's accountant and as a prison ministry organizer.

Sharon **doesn't** miss the aggravation of various external agencies micromanaging her agency's budgets, or having to have duplicate informational meetings so that the board of directors and leadership teams could be separately heard on agency issues and give honest input. "In my retired life, I can be much more honest and open, instead of having to rely constantly on diplomacy as the safest route for communication."

During this retirement transition time, Sharon spends more time with her husband and her friends, continues to volunteer with her church and numerous community alliances and organizations, but recently began to see that simplifying her life was the best approach. "I had felt for a while that, instead of piling on more volunteering as I retired, I should pass on many of those responsibilities to others in the church and community, which would give them the chance to serve their fellow man." She started by cutting out her church choir and nursing home ministry involvement.

Sharon also recognizes that as she gets older, it makes more sense to slow the pace of her activity and involvement. Part of the logic of that approach is so that she can get used to taking the time to really pay attention to her inner voice (which she does by reading the Bible, having a daily prayer time, and listening to worship music), and to center herself for whatever life brings next. For example, she recently felt led to reach out to an older neighbor, is fostering a relationship with her, and is talking to her about faith issues. Also, "There are opportunities to give feedback to my pastor and church council about how to attract younger families to our church."

Sharon suggests that "If you are thinking about retiring, to first have a plan (or three!) and to know what you want to do. Do you want to expand your horizons, or to simplify your life? Do you want to sell your house and travel, or take the time to do home improvements and stick close to home?" She advises that you remain flexible with your plan, so that if health issues or family issues arise, you can change the plan. Sharon and her husband have a foster son whom they know they will be helping financially and otherwise, but they also have had to assist another family member who fell on hard times, and they have left their budget flexible to accommodate unexpected changes. And "even though I am only 65, I am starting to prepare my surroundings and belongings so that if I am suddenly incapacitated or pass away, my family members will not have to worry about more than the funeral arrangements."

Sharon is enjoying her retired life, preparing for the future, and is truly centering herself and at peace with whatever happens next.

Dave Dames: A Comfortable Retirement

Dave Dames is a clean-cut, trim and energetic retiree. He meets me in the suburbs of Pittsburgh at Eat'n'Park, a local chain of homestyle

Americana restaurants. His relaxed and confident personality immediately puts me at ease. He tells me a couple of corny jokes and after we order coffee, begins to share his story.

In many ways, Dave Dames' retirement story is classic: a large insurance corporation experiences major restructuring four or five times, and the dedicated employee goes along for the ride until he reaches a financially feasible exit point. In other ways, Dave's story sheds light on how parental experiences can shape an employee's choices, and how any generation can glean wisdom from the previous one:

"In 1989, my father Ray Dames retired after working 39 years for an energy corporation in southwestern Pennsylvania. Although he could have kept working until age 65, he chose an early exit because of some work environment issues that helped hasten his retirement decision." Because his father's work environment had in some ways worn him down, Dave witnessed first-hand how his father blossomed after retirement: "watching that transformation was incredibly impactful."

When Dave himself started to experience some significant work changes that impacted his own quality of life (including management responsibilities that kept him from performing other project planning that was very important), he started to ruminate on his father's experiences and began to actively plan for - and look forward to - retirement. At the time, he was 57, and had already had been keeping an eye on his retirement plan and had a personal financial planner. For the first time, Dave really started to think about the financial and personal implications of retiring before age 65, and what the benefits could be. Dave had seen other managers and employees stay beyond the point of discomfort, and it had resulted in cynicism and being burnt-out: "I didn't want to be that old crank who stayed on the job."

Dave had worked for the insurance company since 1980, and had seen management trends wax and wane, and corporate restructuring come and go. Sometimes the workplace didn't seem like the place that he had been trained into: "no one, at least that I was familiar with, had worked there that long. All of my previous mentors, and all of the staff I had worked with, were now gone."

From age 57 until age 60, Dave continued in his position, knowing that he wasn't quite financially ready to let go of it. As the stock market bounced up and down, and the American market recession had a very specific impact on his 401k, there were times when Dave felt trapped. "My work/life balance had disappeared around age 55, my workplace started demanding more of my time and energy, but I felt a heavy responsibility to stay. Both my wife and my work team were counting on me. I never felt 100% panicky, but I did have that trapped feeling off and on. I just felt - stuck." Dave was fully experiencing the Disillusionment stage of Fisher's Process, the realization that one's goals and values no longer match those of the organization.

There were also functional and practical reasons why Dave had started to feel that he wasn't working in a familiar workplace. "The demands on our management team because of a shift in our work environment towards bureaucracy and away from a small-business feel: that really impacted the types of demands on our time and how productive we were at the more project-based aspects of our job. When the job tips more than 50% towards management of people instead of projects, you can feel bogged down by paperwork, by proving your job as a manager."

As Dave neared age 60 and experienced less work/life balance, he started making some plans. First, he asked his supervisor to meet with him over coffee so that Dave could propose an elimination of his own position in return for an early retirement. Dave also had his financial planner "run the numbers" on how early Dave could realistically retire, and he touched base often with the planner regarding whether he could retire before 65. Dave was experiencing the Gradual Acceptance stage of Fisher's Process during his retirement transition: "I can see myself in that future, and it holds many good things."

Then Dave met with his supervisor again, to follow up after the first meeting. It made a lot of sense for Dave and for his supervisor to agree to Dave's early retirement: by age 60 Dave would have a full pension and 401k, and his supervisor could eliminate Dave's position from the department budget, which was financially lucrative even after the severance package was factored in. Dave had already realized, through meetings with his financial planner, that he was financially much better off than most people, even though Dave and his wife were a one-income family. That gave Dave the financial confidence to pursue the path to early retirement, and Dave and his supervisor set Dave's official retirement date as December 31, 2012, which eliminated any awkward tax filing transition issue. Dave had progressed to the Moving

Forward stage, in which he was now in control over his future and was confident that he was making the right choice.

Having had almost three years of retirement under his belt, Dave can reflect on why his retirement transition went so smoothly. "I was always able to juxtapose those people who I knew from work whose main identity was their work, and those who saw their work as means to an end. I had noticed over my work experiences that it is better to work to live, than to live to work, and repeated that healthy approach in my own life. Self-mastery of a position was never my identity, and so planning for retirement was a positive experience, its end goal being released from the job."

Achieving a healthy retirement attitude partially comes from Dave's observations of friends who retired well ahead of him, what they did right and how to emulate those steps. It also included making plans with his wife about how best to spend his "spare" time after retirement, to develop good boundaries about how much to be involved in the care of his grandchildren, to share with his men's group any difficulties at work and after retirement, and finding different ways to find fulfillment of his talents and gifts.

There are a few things that Dave misses about his job, including the friendships and camaraderie at work. He still meets some coworkers for lunch occasionally and for social events. He also misses the intellectual challenges that his job offered, including problem-solving and analysis. But there is a longer list of what he doesn't miss: frequent corporate restructuring, changing management trends, office politics, heavy administrative responsibilities, the "rat race" of corporate work, and validation of his performance, to name just a few. Dave DID enjoy his job, most of the time, but was done with corporate life by the time of his retirement.

Dave's advice for any potential retiree is this: "Do an honest assessment of your work identity and how retirement will affect you: where is your identity right now? Take stock, ahead of time, how retirement will affect your marriage and how the roles at home will shift, if that applies to you; retirement can be a challenge as you adjust your home life! Start to examine your finances and plan for retirement WAY ahead of time, not a year before you plan to retire. Set up a plan for how you and your spouse will handle helping with the grandkids. And lastly, find a fun activity that you enjoy that doesn't have to include your spouse, something just your own."

Almost three years after his final day at work, Dave's life is very full and busy, but not "too busy". He volunteers one a day a week at the office of his Christian prayer group. He also coordinates and serves at church services at a nursing home near his home, one day a week, which requires preparation of a short sermon based on the readings from the Bible. The preparation for that has been very spiritually fulfilling for Dave. Dave and his wife have also done a lot of traveling, including a trip to Israel and trips to the national parks throughout the United States. Dave has taken up running for sport, and belongs to a local runners group. He periodically meets with his "old" work friends, who are all former employees of the insurance company. He also enjoys golfing and spending a lot of time with his wife, and looks forward to what God would want him to do next.

Monica Yorke: Adaptation and Acceptance

Monica Yorke is almost 70, always stylishly dressed and freshly coiffed. Whatever some people settle into when they retire (comfortable clothes, caring less about their appearance, white Asic shoes), she doesn't fit the bill. Monica often dresses as if she is still ready to leave for a normal day of work, though she has been retired for five years: dress pants, dress shirt or sweater, pretty scarf, and her makeup always fresh.

"I suppose having to retire early for medical reasons is as good a reason as any, although I would have preferred to get to age 66 ½, which has more financial and logistical advantages. Thankfully, I had already been living pretty simply when the time came."

Monica's path to retirement began sometime in 2000 when the local water treatment company she had been working for as a chemist was suddenly sold off to a French company, and the company laid off the employees and left the Pittsburgh area. One of those employees decided to purchase a soap company building in Monica's hometown, and start a company to formulate and sell soap products. Monica joined that company, and things were good until 9/11 happened: "After the terrorist attacks, many small businesses foundered because the U.S. economy was uncertain for a while. I ended up working for a small water treatment company, at least until 2003, when my employer died. I left a message for a mutual friend to inform him of my boss' death, and that person called me back and offered me a job! From 2004 until 2009, I worked on-site for his company, a boiler-cooling treatment business."

In 2009, a progressive eye condition that Monica had been suffering from for many years suddenly quickly progressed, and she wasn't able to safely drive the 45-minute commute to work. Monica negotiated a contract position with her employer, and worked two or three days per week, sometimes from home. "But my insurance premiums had gotten higher every year, and when ObamaCare really took off in 2010, the small business I was working for took a financial hit for my medical care. My employer graciously agreed to offer benefits to bridge the gap in care until I turned 65, but it really was a financial hardship for him."

In the meantime, Monica was completely blind in one eye, her other eye was floundering, and the doctors researched her condition to try to find a proper diagnosis. "I was sent to several specialists in Pittsburgh at the Eye & Ear Institute, and I was also sent to the Cleveland Clinic for a consultation, to figure out why my sight continued to decline. Once the eye mapping machine was invented, my opthamologist figured out that I had detached aqueous humor disease. It took three years. At the time, they had no useful treatment for it, and the disease kept progressing. Finally, in 2012, my employer asked me to retire, at age 65; my insurance costs had become too prohibitive."

Monica agreed to the early retirement, having taken into consideration the accommodations he had already made for her condition and overall situation: "for three years, he had allowed me to work as a contract employee, many times from home. My friends and neighbors had to drive me to work when I had to go into the office, and I was dependent on the assistance of others to make the situation work. It was time for me to truly retire." Monica had reached the Gradual Acceptance stage of Fisher's Process: she had started to see herself fitting into the construct of her medical situation, and was making peace with the inevitable results of it.

Thankfully, Monica hadn't seen her job as her main identity since her 20's, when she had a sort of personal revelation: "I made a conscious decision to see my work life as means to an end: a way to pay the bills, but my identity is not as an employee first. I had started to see how business worked shortly after I graduated from college: I always saw the field of science as the pursuit of truth, but corporations see science as a power trip, as something to be twisted in the ultimate pursuit of money and power." Monica had also logistically and financially adjusted her life when she began her contract position in 2009. She made the conscious decision to "live more simply." Monica overcame an additional medical crisis in 2009, when she underwent major surgery for a meningioma (non-cancerous tumor) in her spinal column, after she had also been diagnosed with a meningioma in her brain. The surgery, inpatient hospitalization afterwards, and physical therapy for a couple of months afterwards had given her time to think and to get perspective in life. "My prayer group, my community, had offered practical and functional assistance during both of my medical issues, but they were also key to my emotional and spiritual health during those times. My community friends accompanied me through both medical crises, they were always there, especially when I had life restrictions because of balance issues and had to learn how to walk again."

Although Monica didn't see her work life as the core of her identity, there were other considerations that caused her some amount of anxiety about retirement. "As a society, we no longer operate as if families are "tribes"; and because I am single with no children, I had a fair amount of anxiety around who will take care of me when I can no longer care for myself. There is a difference now in how retired or elderly people are seen and perceived, and who is responsible for them. They aren't seen as valuable."

Monica has a set schedule, and an excellent social support network in place that creates stability and mental stimulation for her. Many of her friends retired at or around the same time as Monica, so they share that experience. She participates in local Bible studies and The West Hills Art League, which helps keep her intellectually stimulated. Monica paints for pleasure, using photographs and greeting cards as her subjects. She also serves her church by participating in the choir and Christian Mothers. "Although, I do feel that more could be done in my prayer group to address the identity, lifestyle and schedule changes that occur in retirement, maybe in a more organized way? So many of my community friends are retiring around the same time, we all could use a more organized approach to support."

Monica's focus in retirement is about prioritizing people and relationships. "For single people, that is even more important than for couples. It's more emotionally healthy for us to prioritize people over tasks or functions. It's something that we get out of our jobs before retirement: social contact, intellectual stimulation, and the self-confidence that comes from providing for yourself. That should shift to a more self-driven, conscious decision after retirement, to get out of the house and be active and to see people."

What was Monica happy to leave behind when she retired? "Getting up early! I get up naturally now, unless I have plans. I also was happy to give up the pressure of meeting other people's expectations at work, a/k/a 'the rat race': I don't miss that, at all."

Monica has a lot of advice for other people considering retirement: "Plan, plan, PLAN! About 20 years ahead of time, you should be planning out technical logistics, like how much money it requires and where you want to retire to, but also long-term care insurance. A few years before retirement, you should be figuring out what you want to do with your time afterwards. If you are single, what will your retirement look like?

Secondly, you should take the attitude that retirement is a new adventure, not a purposeless state in life. It's an adventure that should be used for unselfish purposes, working for the spiritual wellbeing of your friends and family. You have time to pray for them and their needs, you can stay in your community and your church and find your "new purpose" there. Maybe you can help the younger families, provide logistical or emotional support for them?

Third, you should take initiative to reach out to others. <u>Choose</u> to be a part of other people's lives. Take an <u>active</u>, not passive role. Relate to people, pray for and with them, show concern for them, and form friendships with other people who are unlike yourself. You still have something to learn from other people."

Monica adds "I am still adjusting to my retirement. I try to keep my schedule regular but not too firm, that way, if some opportunity comes up, I am flexible enough to say yes to it. I have plans to organize my house, donate my extra books, throw away unneeded paperwork, and simplify my life. I stay active, but also available to my friends and family. I'm still figuring it out!"

Phil Milone: Making The Most Of Life

I first meet Phil Milone at the Veterans' Breakfast Club, a local outreach to American soldiers and war veterans. The tall, broad-shouldered and salt-n-pepper retiree agrees to meet with me, not to discuss his adjustment to civilian life, but to tell me about the end of his career. We meet some weeks later at a local Eat'n'Park where Phil greets me (with hearty handshake and a booming voice) for coffee, pie, and a story.

When Phil Milone returned to the states after eight years in the Air Force, including some time in Vietnam during the war and a stint in Japan, he never thought that finding the perfect vocational fit would come from a simple newspaper ad. "There I was, flipping through the want ads in the Pittsburgh Press, and I saw a simple little ad for 'help wanted' from Mosler Safe." Interviewing for that position as a time lock repairman for Mosler touched off a 34-year career with the safe company that Phil enjoyed very much. He traveled all over the region to repair time locks for banks and businesses, and enjoyed his time on the road, the challenge of repairing time locks, and talking to clients.

Thirty-four years into his career, Mosler Safe was suddenly purchased by ADT. Phil stayed another six months with them, and then found a position with Consultech, another local company. He worked for Consultech for nine years until arthritis in his back forced his retirement in 2009. Phil (aged 75) experiences weakness and pain in his legs from the arthritis, but that hasn't stopped him from continuing to volunteer with a civics organization through his Catholic parish. He also volunteers at a local food bank and until recently, helped with the church bereavement committee and a yearly fundraiser.

The aspect of his career that Phil misses the most is the customers and his coworkers, and he has tried to accommodate for by volunteering and fostering friendships. He doesn't miss the constant driving (something that may have caused his back problems in the first place), nor the huge responsibility of drilling safes open without setting the inside contents on fire. Phil is in the Gradual Acceptance stage of the Fisher's Process, with regards to his career identity.

The downturn in Phil's health has affected other aspects of his life as well, and the recent end of a relationship with his girlfriend has left him bewildered and feeling lost. Their mutual friends still talk to Phil, but the activities that Phil used to share with his girlfriend are no longer shared with their peer group.

Phil, now 75, is resolved to make the best of his situation, by continuing to stay active in the community and to spend time with his friends from church, and friends who share his military background. He frequently speaks with one brother who lives in Miami and his sister who lives close by. Because of his back pain, his activity level has dropped significantly and he spends his free time relaxing, watching sports and chatting with friends on the phone. He plans to spend the new year socializing and exercising at the local Jewish Community

Center, making new friends there, and reviving his relationship with his grown daughter and her family.

"My best advice for those who plan to retire is to do the planning ahead of time, to keep busy, and to volunteer in your community; to stay active!"

Bob Tedesco, Sr.: Seasons of Change

"To everything there is a season, and a time to every purpose under heaven:
A time to be born, and a time to die; a time to plant, a time to reap that which is planted;
A time to kill, and a time to heal; a time to break down, and a time to build up;
A time to weep, and a time to laugh; a time to mourn, and a time to dance;
A time to cast away stones, and a time to gather stones together;
A time to embrace, and a time to refrain from embracing;
A time to get, and a time to lose; a time to keep, and a time to cast away;
A time to rend, and a time to sew; a time to keep silence, and a time to speak;
A time to love, and a time to hate; a time of war, and a time of peace."
Ecclesiastes 3:1-8 (NIV Bible)

These words carry the themes of Bob Tedesco, Sr.'s life; that coincidental happenings coincide, but are not accidental. That one decision builds on the next, and the next; that decisions have seasons in our lives, and those seasons arrive, and then leave us.

Upon reflection, Bob's vocational identities take two distinct and coinciding paths: that of a self-disciplined and respected engineer, and that of a self-sacrificing and driven Christian community leader. Not that the descriptions of these attributes are limited to the two distinct vocational paths, but there are themes to each that stand out:

"2002 was my last year of consulting work for Eaton, and it just made no sense for me go and look for another engineering position at the age of 60," says Bob, describing how his consultant work in the field of engineering finally ended. "Eaton bought Westinghouse in the mid-'90's, and steadily started cutting out consultants and contract workers. In a way, it was a compliment to my work that they kept me for so long."

After almost a decade in university while working various jobs and supporting his wife and ten children, Bob began working for

Westinghouse in 1981 as a full-time engineer. He had left his engineering position in 1975 to pursue full-time pastoral work, but in 1980 the recession hit and Bob's pastoral salary became affected, and he had to go back to engineering work. After two years of working 40+ hours a week for Westinghouse, and 20+ hours a week doing pastoral work, the toll on Bob's family life got to be too much. A supervisor at Westinghouse suggested a compromise: that Bob work as a consultant, being paid a high hourly wage and having more control over his work schedule, and Westinghouse would be relieved from providing health, unemployment, and other benefits. Bob decided that the consultant option was the best way to regain more control over his time and energy.

The true heart of Bob's vocational energy was reserved for his pastoral work and leadership in The People of God, a multi-denominational Christian prayer community based in Pittsburgh, Pennsylvania. In 1998, after 25 years and ten months of sacrificing energy, family and personal time, money and effort, retiring from the head coordinator position was both the right move and a little disorienting to Bob. "I realize that new leadership brings in a new set of gifts and ideas, a new pair of fresh eyes and a new perspective; but I was so used to the position that the enthusiastic support of the new coordinator was…interesting." Bob knew that the new leadership could bring the group in a different direction, and it could be nerve-wracking to watch someone else take over where he had left off; he hadn't anticipated the internal resistance he felt at someone else moving into the position that he had held for two and a half decades.

Bob didn't retire from all pastoral work, but transitioned to work on a regional level with an organization that "creates international unity and consistency in ecumenical communities", called the Sword of the Spirit. Fading into the proverbial background of the local community meant a ramping-up of his presence in Christian communities based in Canada, New Jersey, Michigan, and other Eastern states in the U.S. Bob had long recognized that planning work for newer communities was essential to the health of these organizations, and that attention paid to established communities meant higher levels of member satisfaction and perception of support. Bob's lifelong mission had just expanded its boundaries beyond that of local community concerns.

His advice for how to see your vocational path, to discern where to go next? "Your life has a purpose in God and in his kingdom. It changes as you age. If you seek and find it, you will be more comfortable, even if you can only provide prayer support to others at that point."

Now aged 74, Bob sees his role as that of elder, similar to that of Native American elders: they never truly retire, as they continue to pass on their accumulated wisdom, religious beliefs and familial assistance to other tribe members until they die (Lin, 2010). Because of various health issues and concerns about traveling, Bob may not stay in the position of missionary coordinator for much longer, but he will certainly continue his spiritual writings, advice to other coordinators, planning work, and occasional mission trips to new communities.

His retirement plan? "To die with my boots on."

Chapter 9:
"And In Conclusion..."

    These interviews took place over three years, from 2014 - 2017. The subjects ranged from entrepreneurs to stay at home parents, from working-class employees to small business owners, from military veterans to university professors. Christian or atheist, gay or straight, single or married, priest or layperson, many common themes came to the forefront during the writing process:

Vocational Awareness
    Vocation is not just about what you **do**, it's about who you **are**. The subjects of this book, especially those in second careers or returning to the workforce after a long absence, learned some interesting things about themselves during vocational transitions. Among these lessons were identifying their intrinsic values, how to negotiate, how to compromise, when to give up and when to push on.

What is your calling, your passion? What job most perfectly fits into the gifts, talents, training, and energy that you already possess?

Resilience
The Merriam-Webster Dictionary defines resilience as "the ability to recover from, or adjust easily to, misfortune or change." The interview subjects' experiences ranged from forced retirement to normative first careers to trauma-based career transitions, and amidst it, proved that humans are resilient, capable, and not easily broken. What doesn't kill you, makes you stronger.

Complexity
Our interview group reflects the complex and layered experiences of American workers and foreign university students. Their identity prides itself on ingenuity, independence, and fortitude, but herein we also see the Anxiety, Fear, Anger, Guilt, Depression, Hostility, and Moving Forward stages of Fisher's Process of Transition in real time. These traits coexist in the same person, sometimes even at the same time, which beautifully demonstrates the complexity of the employee or student. It's an 'and' concept: we are both strong and a work in progress. We are physical beings, but we are also spiritual, intellectual, emotional and social beings who require care and personal development within a supportive environment.

Disjointed management, toxic or poorly-trained employees, and competitive workplaces foster dysfunction and lose companies their valued employees, which ultimately hurts the whole company. These interviews strongly suggest that having work and university environments that foster interdependence and cooperation are the healthiest places.

Interdependence
Each person's story reflects the myriad of assistance offered (and accepted) during times of vocational transition: mentoring, financial advice, money assistance, social support, spiritual guidance, shelter, friendship, love and compassion. Each of these components comes from the interdependence we all enjoy within the construct of society, especially within the auspices of the family unit. Repeatedly we see the impact of family love and sacrifice. But we also glimpse the interdependence between friends, within churches and support groups,

intertwined into companies and other formal structures. Each person acknowledges, "I could have not done this on my own."

This should serve as an encouragement for the reader to reflect upon what support structures they have in their own lives, and to strengthen those that have become weak or are absent. Because change is coming, and you want to be ready to weather the storm.

Compassion

Compassion is natural for some, but for others, it's a learned skill. The people who participated in this book both received compassion (through second chances, mentoring, forgiveness or practical help in adjusting) and gave compassion (by suffering in silence to help children adjust to divorce, nursing family members through illnesses, forgiving ex-spouses, and giving latitude to harsh or cruel employers). Compassion is defined by Merriam-Webster's Dictionary as "sympathetic consciousness of others' distress together with a desire to alleviate it." In other words, being aware of someone else's pain and deciding to do something about it. If you find yourself lacking compassion, especially in a work environment, ask yourself: "How did my family of origin express compassion? How can I grow in this area? Whom can I look to as an example of compassion? Why is it important to practice compassion in the workplace? What do these people's stories have to teach me about how to practice compassion?"

Empathy

Empathy is the capacity to understand the story of another, and to glean meaning from it. The healthiest work environments and universities are holistic, which means they recognize the meaning of work/life balance, and incorporate caring for the whole person into their mission and vision. Holistic environments honor and acknowledge that their people are physical, emotional, spiritual, intellectual, and social beings. They create cooperative and interdependent environments that are healthy, safe and productive.

Growing in empathy will grow your group's productivity, because empathy builds bridges between employees or fellow students! Empathy, together with compassion and an understanding of resilience, complexity, and interdependence, integrity, dignity and trust will help you to shape your own vocation (as an employee or student) and the vocations of others (as a mentor, employer, or professor).

What do you have to learn from our subjects' stories, what do you have to gain? Who do these stories remind you of: your employer, your employee, your fellow student, your parent, or yourself? Do you recognize that we all have more in common than is different from the 'other'?

Integrity

Integrity is a character trait that dictates what you are willing to do when no one is watching. Integrity in management of employees is whether you can set aside your own ambitions for the good of your employees and ultimately, for the good of the company. Merriam-Webster defines integrity as "firm adherence to a code of especially moral or artistic values; incorruptibility."

As an employee or student, are you incorruptible? If not, why? What changed, and when? What steps can you take to get back to being someone of whom you can be proud?

As a manager, are you full of integrity? Are you the same person in front of your employees, as you are in front of peers, or your own supervisor? If not, why? What changed, and when? What steps can you take to get back to being someone of whom you can be proud?

Dignity

Dignity is defined by Merriam-Webster as "the quality or state of being worthy, honored, or esteemed." How many of these stories reflected an employee's desire to retain dignity in the face of adversity? Of those, how many lost some of their dignity through the experience of being demoted, laid off, fired, or forcibly retired? What is the human cost of being perceived as an acceptable loss? How can you qualify grief, pain, or the loss of dignity? How can a greater awareness of the inherent dignity of every person affect the way that managers 'do business'?

Trust

At each vocational transition, these employees experienced either negative, neutral, or positive feedback from their managers or work teams. Those experiences helped shape the way the employee approached their new workplace, position or role. What has been your role at your past or present companies? Are you trustworthy? Have you ever contributed to someone else's demotion or firing? Have you 'flown under the radar', and thus, avoided confrontation? Or have you boldly stepped forward when you observed workplace harassment, violence, hostile management attributes, or sexual impropriety, and thus helped to improve your company's approaches to these problems?

Do you see yourself in the role of these employees, their managers, their supporters - or their detractors? What are you willing to change today about your approach or attitude? What do stay at home parents have to do to adjust to trust their own judgment, and how can you have work/life balance when your home **is** your work?

The development of safe, positive, and productive work environments is an opportunity for **all** of us, whether CEO, student, stay at home parent, middle management, Human Resources, or entry-level employee. Be part of the opportunity, not part of the problem!

BIBLIOGRAPHY

"Stress and Gender Study" (2011) The American. Evers, A. & Sieverding, M. (2013, August). "Gender differences in long-term predictors of career success", Retrieved from http://pwq.sagepub.com/content/early/2013/09/11/0361684313498071

Fisher, J.M., (2012) "The Process of Transition", Retrieved from www.c2d.co.uk
Graphics and descriptions printed with the verbal consent of author, July, 2015.

Moyle, P. & Parkes, K. (1999, September) "The effects of Transition Stress: a relocation study", Retrieved from https://www.researchgate.net/publication/229893067_The_Effects_of_Transition_Stress_A_Relocation_Study

American Psychological Association (2011), "Stress and Gender". Retrieved from http://www.apa.org/news/press/releases/stress/2011/gender.aspx

Romm, C. (2014, September) "Understanding How Grief Weakens the Body", Retrieved from http://www.theatlantic.com/health/archive/2014/09/understanding-how-grief-weakens-the-body/380006/
www.learnersdictionary.com

Kubler-Ross, E., (1997) "On Death and Dying". New York, NY: Scribner Publishing.

Di Giovanni, J. & Gaffey, C. (2015, March) "The New Exodus: Christians flee ISIS in the Middle East". Retrieved from http://www.newsweek.com/2015/04/03/new-exodus-christians-flee-isis-middle-east-316785.html

Bosrock, M. (1994), "Put Your Best Foot Forward: Asia". St. Paul, MN: International Education Systems Publishing. Retrieved from http://www.ediplomat.com/np/cultural_etiquette/ce_kr.htm

Davis, J. (2016, July) "Teaching ESL: 10 common problems in the classroom" Retrieved from https://owlcation.com/academia/Teaching-ESL-10-Common-Classroom-Problems-and-Solutions

Zong, J. & Batalova, J. (2015, July) "The Limited English Proficient population in the United States". Retrieved from http://www.migrationpolicy.org/article/limited-english-proficient-population-united-states

Smith, J. (2013, May) "7 Tips for young professionals starting a new job". Retrieved from http://www.forbes.com/sites/jacquelynsmith/2013/05/06/7-tips-for-young-professionals-starting-a-new-job/#21aff90b6193

Sheehy, K. (2013, November) "Undergrads around the world face student loan debt". Retrieved from http://www.usnews.com/education/best-global-universities/articles/2013/11/13/undergrads-around-the-world-face-student-loan-debt

Skinner, B.F. (1953) "Science and Human Behavior". New York, NY: The Free Press Publishing.

Brandon, E. (2011, May) "How to cope with a forced retirement". Retrieved from http://money.usnews.com/money/retirement/articles/2011/05/23/how-to-cope-with-a-forced-retirement

Borritz, M. (2010, October) "Work characteristics affect burnout risk in Human Services workers" Retrieved from https://www.acoem.org/Page2Column.aspx?PageID=7392&id=7259

Tronick, E. (1975) "Ed Tronick and the Still Face Experiment". Retrieved from http://scienceblogs.com/thoughtfulanimal/2010/10/18/ed-tronick-and-the-still-face/

Mooney, B. (2013, March) "The scientific proof that sending mothers out to work harms children". Retrieved from http://www.dailymail.co.uk/femail/article-2296567/Scientific-proof-stay-home-mothers-benefit-children-So-coalition-Budget-tax-break-working-mothers.html

Douglas-Gabriel, D. (2015, July) "Parents are relying more on their earnings - rather than loans - to pay for college". Retrieved from https://www.washingtonpost.com/news/get-there/wp/2015/07/21/parents-are-relying-more-on-their-earnings-rather-than-loans-to-pay-for-college/

Richardson, S. (2014, December) "Finding work/life balance in the darkroom of the soul". Retrieved from http://www.newsworks.org/index.php/local/humanatwork/75970-finding-work-life-balance-in-the-darkroom-of-the-soul

Ceniza-Levine, C. (2013, February) "The only good reason to quit your job". Retrieved from http://www.forbes.com/sites/work-in-progress/2013/02/18/the-only-good-reason-to-quit-your-job/#74055c267c3d

Layton, L. (2014, June) "How Bill Gates pulled off the swift Common Core revolution". Retrieved from https://www.washingtonpost.com/politics/how-bill-gates-pulled-off-the-swift-common-core-revolution/2014/06/07/a830e32e-ec34-11e3-9f5c-9075d5508f0a_story.html?utm_term=.e72ec6a9fa79

LaPonsie, M. (2016, March) "5 Financial tips for military members transitioning to civilian life". Retrieved from http://money.usnews.com/money/personal-finance/articles/2016-03-24/5-financial-tips-for-military-members-transitioning-to-civilian-life

Link, G. & Hepburn, K. (2017, February) "Caregiver Stress". Retrieved from http://www.womenshealth.gov/publications/our-publications/fact-sheet/caregiver-stress.html

Caridi, C. (2009, November) "Can a priest ever return to the lay state?". Retrieved from http://canonlawmadeeasy.com/2009/11/12/can-a-priest-ever-return-to-the-lay-state/

Bluethmann, J. (2015, January) "Losing a spouse: Moving forward as an only parent" Retrieved from http://www.metroparent.com/daily/parenting/parenting-issues-tips/losing-spouse-moving-forward-parent/

Weiten, W., Lloyd, M.A., Dunn, D., & Hammer, E. (2016) "Psychology Applied to Modern Life: Adjustment in the 21st Century"; Cengage Learning, Boston, MA.

Caprino, K. (2013, June) "5 Ways to tell if you need a career change". Retrieved from https://www.forbes.com/sites/kathycaprino/2013/06/20/5-ways-to-tell-if-you-need-a-career-change/#51402d0e2bfa

Global Affairs Canada: "Cultural Information: Philippines", 2017. Retrieved from https://www.international.gc.ca/cil-cai/country_insights-apercus_pays/ci-ic_ph.aspx?lang=eng)

Kramer, K. (August, 2015), "Single mothers much more likely to live in poverty than single fathers, study finds". Retrieved from http://phys.org/news/2015-08-mothers-poverty-fathers.html

Banschick, M., M.D. (February, 2012) "The High Failure Rate of Second and Third Marriages" Retrieved from https://www.psychologytoday.com/blog/the-intelligent-divorce/201202/the-high-failure-rate-second-and-third-marriages

Landers, J. (November, 2011) "Study Shows Divorced Women Have Less Economic Security Than Women Who Stay Married" http://www.forbes.com/sites/jefflanders/2011/11/01/study-shows-divorced-women-have-less-economic-security-than-women-who-stay-married/#67349c8039b6)

Reilly, K. (Spring, 2009) "The Economic Consequences of Divorce: The Role of Child Support, Labor Force Participation and Means Tested Transfers Over Time". Retrieved from https://ecommons.cornell.edu/bitstream/handle/1813/14235/Kristen ReillyFinalThesis1 pdf;sequence=2.

Hershey, D., Ph.D., Henkens, K., Ph.D. (February, 2013) "Impact of Different Types of Retirement Transitions on Perceived Satisfaction with Life" Gerontologist 54 (2):232-244 Retrieved from https://academic.oup.com/gerontologist/article/54/2/232/634390/Impact-of-Different-Types-of-Retirement

Szinovacz, M., Ph.D., Davey, A., Ph.D. (February, 2005) "Predictors of Perception of Involuntary Retirement" Gerontologist 45 (1):36-47 Retrieved from https://academic.oup.com/gerontologist/article/45/1/36/631693/Predictors-of-Perceptions-of-Involuntary

Lin, J. (January, 2010) "Honor or Abandon: Societies' Treatment of Elderly Intrigues Scholar" Retrieved from http://newsroom.ucla.edu/stories/jared-diamond-on-aging-150571

Kotlikoff, L. (June 2015) "Are you getting a fair divorce? The economist's take" Retrieved from http://www.pbs.org/newshour/making-sense/getting-fair-divorce-economists-take/

Landers, J. (March 2017) "FAQ: Bedrock Divorce" Retrieved from https://www.bedrockdivorce.com/faq.php
https://bipartisanpolicy.org/blog/millennials-in-retirement-demographic-shift/

Made in the USA
Middletown, DE
24 November 2018